TELLING PEOPL

For a complete list of Management Books 2000 titles,
visit our web-site on www.mb2000.com

> The original idea for the 'In Ninety Minutes' series was
> presented to the publishers by Graham Willmott, author
> of 'Forget Debt in Ninety Minutes'. Thanks are due to
> him for suggesting what has become a major series to
> help business people, entrepreneurs, managers,
> supervisors and others to greatly improve their personal
> performance, after just a short period of study.

Other titles in the 'in Ninety Minutes' series are:

Forget Debt in 90 Minutes
Understand Accounts in 90 Minutes
Working Together in 90 Minutes
25 Management Techniques in 90 Minutes
Supply Chain in 90 Minutes
Practical Negotiating in 90 Minutes
Find That Job in 90 Minutes
Budgeting in 90 Minutes
Telling People in 90 Minutes
Perfect CVs in 90 Minutes
Networking in 90 Minutes
Payroll in 90 Minutes
… other titles will be added

The series editor is James Alexander

Submissions of possible titles for this series or for management books in
general will be welcome. MB2000 are always keen to discuss possible new
works that might be added to their extensive list of books for people who
mean business.

Creative ideas about achieving a far better level of communication with others, wherever and whenever the need arises

TELLING PEOPLE in 90 Minutes

Libby Hammond and Kim Walker

2000

First published in 2005 by Management Books 2000 Ltd
Forge House, Limes Road
Kemble, Cirencester
Gloucestershire, GL7 6AD, UK
Tel: 0044 (0) 1285 771441
Fax: 0044 (0) 1285 771055
E-mail: info@mb2000.com
Web: www.mb2000.com

Printed and bound in Great Britain by Digital Books Logistics Ltd of Peterborough

British Library Cataloguing in Publication Data is available

ISBN 1-85252-502-9

Contents

To:

On the Hammond side, Natalie and Tom (learning to communicate as the fabulous Harmer newly-weds), Peter (who can talk his way through any situation) and Dick who can talk into the heart with his wisdom.

On the Walker side, Ross and Lyn for their openness of communication and their unconditional love.

Acknowledgements

We are delighted to thank our families for their support as we put this book together. Particular thanks to James Alexander for going with our crazy ideas. And finally, a special thanks to the fabulous singer, songwriter and multi-talented Lucinda Sieger, for the great cartoons.

Foreword

One of the greatest problems facing human beings is the extreme trickiness of letting other people know exactly what you want them to know. You may say to yourself, 'But *I know* exactly what I mean.' Arrogant or what? The majority of conflicts and disputes, shouting matches and stony silences, inter-personal and international arguments, late evening punch-ups and kids' squabblings can be put down to the inability of the protagonists to muster the skill to tell it correctly or to take the time to find the best way to do it.

This book is a welcome and refreshing way to look at the business of telling people, and, if followed closely, will result in far better understanding of the way to give - and, by inference, to receive - information to other people. It is a useful addition to the 'in 90 Minutes' series of books.

Having spent many working years engaged in the business of helping people to improve their communications skills, I must agree with the two writers that the critical factors are preparation and presentation, even if the first is done at speed and on the hoof. Taking a moment to consider how to tell it will save much heartache and avoid much confusion. This is not to say that spontaneity is dangerous, because a skilled 'teller' will have internalised the processes and will always do it right, even under stress.

Read this book and go forth and communicate like a good'un.

James Alexander

Introduction

In 1999, a Gallup Poll produced results that were staggering. The figures were based on a global survey of businesses and revealed that:

- 17% of employees were actively engaged at work
- 67% were at work but not engaged
- and the remaining 16% were neither at work nor engaged!

In their book *'Now, Discover Your Strengths'* Marcus Buckingham and Donald Clifton shared that, in a survey of more than 1.7 million employees in 101 companies from 63 countries, only 20% of respondents felt they had the opportunity to work out of their strengths. Not surprisingly those companies only worked at 20% of their potential.

Whilst we all have different strengths, skills and talents, there is one area that we can all learn to use with amazing results – the way we talk to each other!

Great communication can be learned and is reflected in the relationships within an organisation. Whether you work for yourself or are part of a larger organisation, if the communications skills are great, so will be your business. Companies who put a priority on affirming their people and are committed to enhancing the people element of their business are guaranteed to grow.

There are two images which sum up the difference between excellent communication skills, which creates business growth, and the kind of incompetent communication which sabotages everything you are trying to achieve.

The first image is the anthill. Hundreds of thousands of workers in a thriving society who have the security of knowing:

- **connected value** – commonality and clarity reflected by the formal position held within the culture and good working relationships
- **who is in charge** – the recognised leader: skills and experience
- what **targets** are to be met – e.g. productivity, shareholder profit
- what **decisions** are being made
- 'company' **policy** – clearly articulated strategy and objectives
- room to help new workers find their **role** in the 'big picture'.

To an ant, each one is effective in what it is doing because of the excellent internal two-way communication running from the head of the colony to the workers building the anthill and back again. **They are talking to each other.**

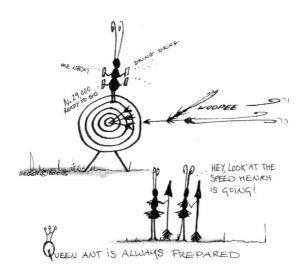

The other image is that of the **Tower of Babel**. It all started off so well until groups encountered the effects of having:

- **dis'connected' value** – individuals doing their own thing with little sense of belonging to a team
- **mismanaged leadership** – lack of accountability and responsibility
- lost contact with other 'departments' – **no targets** combined with increasing isolation, lack of relationships and a real sense of doing your own thing
- **lack of decision-making** resulting in miscommunicated ideas and instructions
- **no company policy** – no acceptable standards of behaviour, resulting in bad attitudes, team breakdown and so on
- **no room for new workers** – that only increased the suspicion and confusion

The chaos that developed, ultimately because of disastrous communication skills, culminated in an organisation that went into liquidation leaving an empty building as a monument to communication chaos.

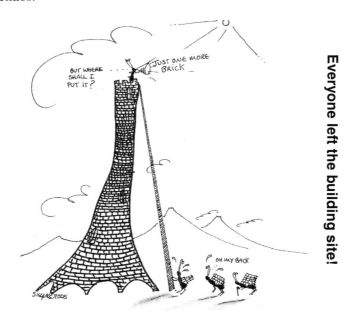

Everyone left the building site!

11

Whether you are in business for yourself or part of a large organisation, this book will cover key principles of communication and how they apply.

> *'Everything you do or say is public relations.'*
>
> Unknown

95% of business growth comes from word of mouth referral, because people buy the person they deal with, the product is secondary. In short, if the client trusts you, they'll buy your product. Every aspect of talking to people is covered in this book and will be highly useful to wooing and winning business, and the great thing is, these principles will also be highly useful at a personal level.

(See two great MB2000 books – *The Hottest Ideas in Word-of-Mouth Advertising*, by Godfrey Harris, and *People Don't Buy What You Sell – They Buy What You Stand For* by Martin Butler)

In other chapters we'll look at how lessons can be learned from the communication mistakes of Enron:

- the need for trust, openness and honesty

- the need for an open culture

- the need to respect each other within a leadership team

- the need to recognise others strengths or expertise and make use of them – talk each other 'up'

- the need to act on what is discussed rather than sweeping things under the carpet.

There is a well known law, the Law of Diminishing Deceit, which runs something like this: the higher up in an organisation someone goes, the more they have to conceal what really is going on from those who are below them. This tends to create a Babel dynamic – at best, confusion and at worst, suspicion.

When excellent communication skills are used, this Law ceases to be applied – the anthill is growing fast!

We will look at the true purpose of communication – how to influence rather than make a noise! We will highlight communication etiquette both formally; meetings, minutes, emails, voicemails, and informally; handling difficult situations, difficult people.

It will highlight good and bad practice, giving really practical tips that will ensure each individual, department, team and business functions at its very best.

'Communication is not a meeting of words – it is a meeting of meaning.'

1

The Art of Communication

There are certain things that have to be understood in order to engage in effective communication. We live in a world where we have become over-reliant on technology as a means of communication: computers, voicemails, emails, text messages, memos, business cards and so on. We haven't always got time to think about what we say or how we come across. Whilst nowadays we are communicating more, and going on courses to practise our interpersonal skills, paradoxically, our verbal communication skills can still be weak. It is not enough to say what we think or share ideas, if we are simply using words as a means of telling others what is on our mind. We need to understand the **art of communication** - how to *influence* others with what we are saying and, to know how to *listen* to others to hear what they are saying. What we hear and how we interpret it affects both our response and the ensuing choices we make.

In this chapter we will cover the key skills needed for the art of communication, giving examples of what is good practice and what should be avoided. But first of all, let's look at the three main types of communicators we come across.

SIEGEL ©2005

Explorers, Scientists and Zoo-keepers

Explorers

These people finds it difficult to keep boundaries with people. They set out to communicate one thing but are happy to get side-tracked if it helps them understand the bigger picture. They want to get to know the area they are dealing with and have plenty of time for the natives. They engage with the people but have to watch they don't get too distracted by other things. As communicators, they have time, emotional energy and genuine passion for their subject but can trample over others feelings and not necessarily listen if their attention is elsewhere.

 Exercise A: What are the advantages and disadvantages of this type of communicator?

(See end of chapter for answers)

Scientists

These people want information, knowledge and more facts. They find it hard to influence as they are more process and performance centred. This doesn't mean they don't communicate with passion about their subject, simply that they seem less emotionally engaged. If what they are doing doesn't work, then it's easier to handle if they stay detached. As communicators, they'll think before they talk and be interested in what is being discussed rather than the people in the conversation.

 Exercise B: What are the advantages and disadvantages of this type of communicator?

(See end of chapter for answers)

Zoo-keepers

These types make sure feeding time and so on goes like clockwork but have little or no time to listen to the needs of individual animals as there is so much to look after. They communicate what needs to be done, engage as much as possible but can only sustain short conversations, otherwise work won't get done. They like group consensus so might say contradictory things so as to please everyone. Not so comfortable with individuals as it might get too intense.

✎ **Exercise C:** What are the advantages and disadvantages of this type of communicator?

(See end of chapter for answers)

✎ **What communication type are you?**

		Yes	No
1	I always think before I talk	☐	☐
2	I like asking questions	☐	☐
3	I learn something new through conversations	☐	☐
4	I am a good active listener	☐	☐
5	I usually end conversations	☐	☐
6	I am aware of when the other person has finished saying what they want to say	☐	☐
7	I feel comfortable with silences	☐	☐
8	I always get the outcome I expect	☐	☐
9	I can make small talk when necessary	☐	☐
10	I am aware of how others are feeling	☐	☐
11	I have a mental check-list of what to cover	☐	☐
12	The more people the merrier	☐	☐
13	I prefer to have everything on paper	☐	☐
14	I highly rate my listening skills	☐	☐
15	I like to summarise what I've heard	☐	☐

Having looked at the three communication types and answered the quiz – which type do you think you are?

Irrespective of whichever type you came up with, there are four key skills needed for the art of communication. We'll give examples of what is good practice and what should be avoided so you can get a feel for these in practise. These four key areas – **boundaries, listening, engaging** and **influencing** – are crucial at every level in business.

1. Boundaries

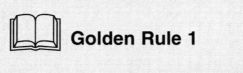

Golden Rule 1

It is better to say nothing, than to witter, unless of course, you can witter with conviction!

a) How to avoid verbally 'putting your foot in it'

Boundaries are a great way of ensuring verbal self-control and determining what choices we make about our behaviour – verbal and non-verbal. They also help put people at their ease as our communication style lets them know who they are dealing with.

What do we mean by boundaries? Put simply, it is a set of principles and practices that we adopt to safeguard ourselves – and those we interact with – from harm. For example, we might choose to be comfortable with silences. Another example is we might decide that we will not use disrespectful language with others and also, that we will not allow others to use disrespectful words with us on the basis that, *'A gentle tongue is a tree of life but perverseness in it breaks the spirit'* Proverbs 15:4.

In practice, that would mean exercising verbal self-control when provoked and responding in a different way. This approach protects us from putting our foot in it and at the same time we help others avoid doing the same with us!

In one organisation I worked in, I had a deputation from another part of the building because there had been a problem with delegate lists. The two ladies were very irate and made it very clear who was to blame and so on. Rather than take a position, I waited until they had finished, thanked them and then said, 'I really appreciated what you've shared and I'll see what I can do, but just one question, were you aware of how you were talking?' Their jaws dropped. They had clear ideas on what they wanted to communicate (which involved walking all over my boundary walls) but had no idea of how they were coming across (they'd stepped over their own walls).

 Exercise: List four principles and practices you want to put in place as part of your communication style.

---

b) Keeping your own counsel

Remember Golden Rule 1! In business, there are those whose communication style is like that of a gossip: asking questions that seem relevant but feel too inquisitive. In trying to seem helpful but not give too much away, we can witter or worse, give confidential information away about a situation, a person or company strategy. A key skill is to learn to *deflect* the line of conversation onto safer ground, which in effect, strengthens your boundaries.

Deflection tips when asked an intrusive question:

'That's a very good question but I think we should be focussing on ...'
'Why is ... of particular interest to you?'
'I'd need to reflect a bit more on that before giving an answer'

'Excellent question and I'll come back to that later – but what I'd like to know is ...'

Or the very reliable,

'Oh, I see coffee has arrived – let me get you a cup.'

c) Reading the danger signals in someone's body language

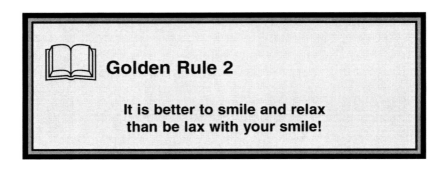

Golden Rule 2

It is better to smile and relax than be lax with your smile!

This is very straightforward. If the people you are talking with are shifting from one foot to the other, twiddling and doodling with their paperwork, avoiding eye contact with you, or the smile they give doesn't reach their eyes, engagement has been lost and the conversation needs to end. A way of ending this is to say, for example, 'I think we've covered everything at the moment so let's take a break' or 'Any questions at this stage?' Creating a break changes the energy dynamic and is a good way of re-engaging. A good book to refer to is *'Is there a Speaker in the Room?'* by Libby Hammond as this covers reading body language in more depth.

d) Striking the balance between familiarity and over-familiarity

Boundaried physical behaviour is really important. If you leap up to greet someone who may be suffering from depression, with a big smile and a 'Hi, I'm … it's fantastic to meet you', and an enthusiastic handshake, you might put them off continuing the conversation. Some people don't like being touched, or being treated like your best friend if it's the first time you've met.

Just imagine putting up wallpaper. The wall is ready, the paper pasted, but you gently put the paper against the wall until it is in the right position. Then you brush it firmly into place checking that everything is okay as you go along. Any creases will gently ease away and the paper will dry perfectly.

2. Listening

Communication is not a meeting of words, it's a *meeting of meaning*.
How do you learn to *hear* what someone is saying?

a) Having a meeting of meaning

It is easy to jump in with an answer or opinion on what has been said. The secret to learning what someone means is very simple – ask questions. We're referring to questions that give more understanding of what the person means. For example, someone might say: 'The paper isn't ready for printing'. What they might mean by that is that the computer has crashed or the secretary hasn't finished typing it or the printer is out of commission. What you might imagine in your mind is that someone has been unprepared and caught short! Simply asking 'Why isn't it ready?' gives an opportunity for a meeting of meaning and defuses a potential conflict situation.

Golden Rule 3

Ask who, what, why, where and when questions to save misunderstandings - better a meeting of meaning than a clash of attitudes !

b) Patience

Avoid the goldfish approach – mouth opening and closing to indicate that something is waiting to come out! The best business deals are struck by people who have learned to wait until the other person has finished speaking. Why? They have learned more by listening than by speaking. They have observed body language, tone of voice and content. They have sought for a meeting of meaning and were willing to be quiet to hear what was being said and not just wait for a gap in the conversation to get in their own bit. God gave us two ears and one mouth – we should try to use them in that proportion. Patience also helps you to focus with intent so that you can adjust your strategy according to what you hear.

 Exercise: Watch 10 minutes of a favourite programme. List all the observations you can make about people's communication styles. How many have you noted?

(See end of chapter for score)

'You can learn a lot from people who view the world differently than you do.'

Anthony D'Angelo

3. Engaging

The most powerful instant communicator is our body language (remember Golden Rule 2). In terms of initially engaging with anyone, how we smile as we shake hands means all the difference between the individual trusting us or not.

Good body language = easy relationships = easy conversations.

Remember people buy you not your product. If they like you (and that is established subconsciously within the first couple of minutes), you have an open door to presenting your product. There are some really excellent examples of opening sentences and questions that act as a precursor to taking the conversation to a level that should result in business being transacted.

Some good opening gambits

- Hi, I'm .... How was your journey across?

- Can I introduce myself. I'm ... Did the weather spoil/was the weather good over the weekend?

- Which way did you come here? Was the traffic quiet/busy at that time of day?

- You seem to be the outdoor type - what is your hobby? or 'Oh,you don't like sport - how do you manage to look so fit?

When we are nervous we can end up either talking about ourselves, what we do and, worse, overdosing on how amazing we are, or we go the other route of grilling the person we're talking to. If you keep 'other-centred' you'll automatically ask the kind of questions that give you an understanding of who you're with. Keep what you have to say succinct – which means having thought beforehand what you'd like to say. The American's refer to 'elevator pitch' techniques and we'll touch on those when we cover networking in a later chapter.

If you put your foot in it, the best thing is to stay relaxed and either apologise, if that's appropriate, or, move on quickly without drawing attention to what's been said.

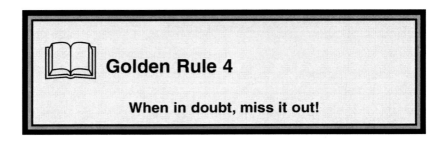

Golden Rule 4

When in doubt, miss it out!

The most influential way of signalling you are actively listening is by good eye contact, verbal affirmations, e.g. 'uh-huh', 'yes', 'is that so?' and so on. The easiest way of making your contribution is not by leaping in at the first pause. Rather, watch the other person and listen to what he or she is saying. When she stops, pause and wait to see if she wants to say anything more, then speak. If you are with a marathon talker, and you have to engage with her (a possible business deal or you've been asked to look after her), then fix her intently in the eye and when she gets disconcerted, stop – then start your contribution to the conversation. Guaranteed to work!

'Tact is the art of making a point without making an enemy.'
Unknown

4. Influencing

Remember what we said at the beginning of this chapter – people buy a person, not their product – and so understanding yourself and others is a key to gauging what to say and how to keep boundaries. So how do we create the kind of influence that guarantees a win-win outcome?

a) Know yourself and have a speaking style that reflects your strengths

If you are good at telling stories and jokes, then use that to help engage in a conversation. If not, don't! There is nothing that kills the dynamics in a conversation more than a poorly told joke – especially if it's drawn out, the punchline only serving to bring to an end the tortuous listening process. However, help is at hand as if you're not good at telling jokes – a great quotation can illustrate the point beautifully. If you are a quick thinker, you will probably speak quite quickly to communicate your rapidly developing ideas. Plan to speak slower so that you can use this to emphasise and make your point. Focusing on your breathing is a great way to slow down your speech.

Some examples of speaking style strengths would be: appropriate use of humour, being succinct, being good at asking questions, articulate, easy with pauses, not too fast, and relaxing to listen to. Have a go at the next exercise and see if you can list at least six aspects of your own speaking style.

✍ **Exercise:** List your speaking style strengths.

---

b) Learn to put yourself in your audience's shoes.

When you are listening to your fellow conversationalist, you are reacting positively or negatively to his or her body language, style of speech, content. You are forming an opinion of that person as an individual and gauging where you want to take the conversation – to introduce your business, influence buy-in on a project you're working on or whatever. So is the other person. If you step into your audience's shoes and think about what he is hearing you say, how might that affect what you say and how you say it? We'll cover more of this in the next chapter.

c) Be aware of your body language and boundaries

This was covered earlier in the chapter.

d) Good use of eye contact and voice tone

The art of influencing with our communication style is like listening to an orchestra. Do you like listening to a monotonous note stretched out for half-an-hour, or sudden strident rises in volume.

Exercise: Listen to the way people on the radio sound. How do they use tone of voice to illustrate or emphasise what they are saying. List what you observe. Tape yourself reading from a newspaper article. List the different ways you used voice tone - how do you compare?

e) Be sensitive in your communication

It is better to compromise and win long-term relationships than win the point and lose the conversation along with any the business opportunity. Are you easily riled by issues or like to win the point – beware!

> *'Your temper is one of your most valuable possessions.*
> *Don't lose it.'*
>
> Anon

Chapter 1 – Exercise answer page

Exercise A:

Advantages: This person would be creative, people-centred (a magnet for others), have subject matter knowledge, risk-taker, stickability in relationships

Disadvantages: Might be difficult to influence because of firm views, easily distracted, might not respect boundaries, might make snap decisions that are not so well thought through.

Exercise B:

Advantages: Gets the job done, doesn't let emotions get in the way, communicates a strategy, most likely good at reflecting and so are well-considered in their views

Disadvantages: Might have difficulty building relationships and engaging people, don't empathise so well, don't influence and might appear unfeeling

Exercise C:

Advantages: Everyone knows him – high visibility, gets the job done and is clear about how it should be done, involves groups and delegates

Disadvantages: Individuals might not have freedom to speak out, could be perceived as dictatorial, limited empathy

Exercise D:

< 10   Practise a lot
10 – 25   Average
> 25   Very observant

2

The Purpose of Communication –

'How to Influence Rather Than Make a Noise'

Communication is universally recognised as the key to successful relationships (personal and business) and much attention is given to developing our interpersonal skills. The area of written communication however is often overlooked as a key way to engage and influence. The success of any communication is measured by the ability to get your message across and influence the recipient rather than just make a noise.

This chapter will look at the breadth of communication tools we have available to us through the written word.

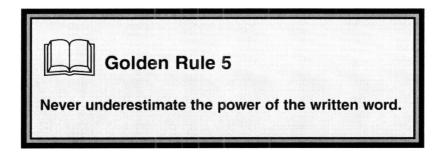

Golden Rule 5

Never underestimate the power of the written word.

The ants are successful at building their anthill because their communication is structured in a way that is easily understood by all. We consider the lessons from this and look at ways to construct our written work and how to structure our communication by maximising the beginning, middle and end.

Most of us have a preference for verbal communication – it tends to be more natural and, of course, we have the opportunity to talk everyday. In business, everything that is discussed eventually ends up on paper. Written documentation is essential to keeping everything clear and in order. So how do we influence using the written word?

Timing

To create maximum impact, the method of communication is important and so too is the timing.

The importance of timing of communication ...

Three friends were enjoying a day out at the races, a plumber, a miner and a bookmaker's clerk. Unfortunately, one of the horses went berserk, jumped over the rails, killing the miner. His two friends were devastated and they decided that the right thing for them to do was to tell his wife. They were nervous so they decided to write her a note. But, who would deliver it? They drew straws and the bookmaker's clerk made his way to her house. He knocked on the door of his dead friend's home. A woman answered. 'Is widow Smith there?' he asked. The woman replied, 'There's no widow Smith here, I'm Mrs Smith ...' 'Do you want to make a bet ...?' asked the bookmakers clerk!

The right message but the wrong messenger ...

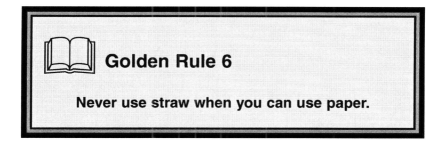

Golden Rule 6

Never use straw when you can use paper.

Fortunately, in this chapter, the paper is the *right* messenger.

1 – Understand the recipient

'Good management is the art of making problems so interesting and their solutions so constructive that everyone wants to get to work and deal with them.'

Paul Hawken

This quote summarises the challenge of communication and especially written communication to share passion, engage and enthuse the recipient. As the story of the three friends shows, successful communication relies upon careful preparation.

Firstly understand your recipients – consider the people who will read your communications and try to put yourself in their shoes and aim to see things as they would see them. When you are preparing a presentation, you think about your relationship with your audience. You establish rapport, create interest, say what you are going to say. Then you say it. The same principles apply to written communication.

✍ Exercise A: Recipient Exercise

When thinking of any written communication you are going to deliver, how would you answer the following questions:

1. Is what is written likely to receive the full attention of the reader? If not, why not?

2. Is the recipient a fast or slow reader?

3. Is the recipient an emotional or logical thinker?

4. Is it aimed at an individual or group of people?

5. If a group of people are receiving the communication, what does that mean in terms of your message?

(See end of chapter for answers)

In appropriate circumstances, engagement of the reader can be increased by using the reader's name in the body of the text. It not only draws the reader's attention, it demonstrates that you are thinking about the person to whom the communication is addressed.

2 – The big picture – influence

a) Content

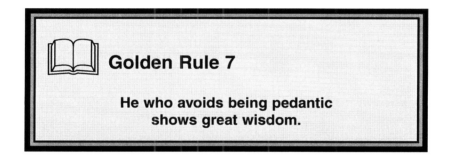

Golden Rule 7

**He who avoids being pedantic
shows great wisdom.**

Once you have thought about the recipient, you can concentrate on influencing the content. Therefore you need to be clear on:

- purpose (why am I writing this)
- what is it that you want to say
- what is the outcome you require.

Stephen R Covey, author of *The 7 Habits of Highly Effective People,* says you must start with the end in mind. A clear structure facilitates brevity and allows your message to be heard rather than to be lost in a noise of words.

As a part of your preparation, it is useful to draft a brief summary of the facts with comments and then make sure they fit within the following format. A good guide is to have:

- a **single purpose** which is best placed at the beginning of the communication
- **no more than three key points** forming the middle of the communication
- detail about the **outcome** you require as the ending.

Keep in mind that the aim is to engage your reader not send them to sleep!

 Exercise:

Think of introducing yourself to a new client or someone you have not met before. In no more than 50 words cover:

→ beginning

→ middle

→ end.

Give it to someone else to review, and ask, can they clearly identify the beginning, middle and end.

Keep sentences short, comprehensible and clear. If you go on too long, there is a danger the reader will forget the beginning before reaching the end. Break down your sentences to avoid breaking down your reader's attention span!

 Golden Rule 8

Better to break down your sentences than give your readers a breakdown!

34

Choose words that are in common usage. This results in your communication being quicker to read and easier to understand. An independent organisation, the Plain English Campaign, has been set up to encourage communication to be produced in crystal clear language.

As part of the recommendations, they suggest that we use alternatives to some of the words that are common in business language; e.g. use:

- **'Try'** instead of 'attempt'

- **'About'** instead of 'concerning'

- **'For'** instead of 'in respect of'

- **'About'** instead of 'regarding'

- **'End'** instead of 'terminate'

✍ Exercise: Spot the deliberate mistake …

1. Ancient Egypt was inhabited by mummies and they all wrote in hydraulics. They lived in the Sarah Dessert. The climate of the Sarah is such that all of the inhabitants used to live elsewhere.

2. Queen Elizabeth was the 'Virgin Queen,' as a queen she was a success. When she exposed herself to her troops they all shouted 'hurrah.'

3. The Greeks were a highly sculptured people, and without them we wouldn't have history. The Greeks also had myths. A myth is a female moth.

4. The third verse of Blessed Assurance will be sung without musical accomplishment.

It is common in business to embrace *jargon* and *acronyms* as a shorthand language. This aids the pace of communication but does rely upon the understanding of the receiver. If in doubt, avoid their use or explain and clarify meaning.

b) Influence – getting 'buy in'

Written communication should aim to engage the recipient at an emotional level to get his or her attention. This technique is used by many marketing companies in advertising campaigns. For example, advertising for cosmetics or fragrance aims to make us believe that, by not using the product, we will not be socially acceptable or attractive.

Communications that contain over complex vocabulary or are peppered with jargon can lead the reader to feel inferior, frustrated or angry. In these circumstances, the message is lost.

c Influence – style

The style of language in written communication is more important than it is in verbal communication. In verbal communication, we have the benefit of seeing and/or hearing the reaction and we can modify our style in response. The same opportunity does not exist in written communication.

Generally, there are three written styles:

- **Chatty** is a very familiar and relaxed style usually adopted for personal communications. The style is only used in business circumstances where there is a strong relationship in place and even then is usually restricted to a couple of paragraphs, usually the opening and closing.

- **Directional style**, as the name suggests, is much more autocratic. It is used in circumstances where you want the reader to 'do as I say'. This style portrays a parent:child relationship. It is a style that is appropriate when there is a need to give instructions or where the writer has specific expertise, e.g. a lawyer may use this style to good effect.

- **Coaching style** is more democratic, encouraging and supportive. It is aimed at helping receivers come to their own conclusion or decision through influence and persuasion. This is most commonly used in marketing literature.

As we mentioned earlier in the section about getting buy-in, communication should aim to engage, and adopting the right style can enhance the reader's interest and engagement,

---

✎ **Exercise B:**

Pause a moment and consider what writing style you use most effectively.

Describe when you might use each style:

- chatty
- directional
- coaching

(See end of chapter for answers)

Each of us is an individual – we are all unique. Any sales person quickly realises the value of relationships in that as consumers, we buy from people. It is important for the salesperson to establish rapport, empathy and portray openness and honesty. In business, we often suppress our personality in written communication by using language that we would never use if we were talking. The way we speak and the language we use tells a lot about us ... be yourself.

'There is only one corner of the universe that you can be certain of improving, and that's your own self.'
Aldous Huxley

Golden Rule 9

Let your personality smile through your pen.

There is a great opportunity for each of us to improve our written communication. We can simply observe and replicate the work of others or we can choose to let our personalities shine through. It is easy for us to improve by critically reviewing written materials and adopting what we think are good and effective styles. At the same time, recognising and avoiding those which are less effective.

✍ **Exercise:**

Review each of the paragraphs below - which style do you prefer and why?

1.

When it comes to preparing for a talk, there is no substitute for hard work and a well prepared brief. The speaker that prepares well and matches his content to the desired briefing outcomes will always land safely. So assuming you've prepared your basic material, let's look at getting that safe landing.

Taken from *'Is There a Speaker in the Room?'* by Libby Hammond

2.

Accounting is a language that is used to store and communicate economic information about organisations. It has a set of rules, which have emerged through practice rather than as a result of an exercise to decide what is the best approach. It is particularly important that anyone trying to read accounting statements and draw conclusions from them is clear on the rules of accounting. Severe misunderstandings could arise for someone not familiar with the rules reading accounting statements.

Taken from *'Business Finance, Theory and Practice'* by EJ McLaney

---

Chapter 2 – Exercise answer page

Exercise A

1. This is a critical question to ask yourself. Having read your communication, if the answer is no or you are unsure, you should refer to section 2 on influence.
2. If the recipient is a fast reader, he or she will generally respond well to a longer communication. If the recipient is a slow reader, keep sentences and paragraphs short so that the main points are clear and you do not risk the reader becoming bored.
3. If the recipient is an emotional thinker consider using language which will appeal to him, i.e. descriptive language that stimulates feelings. If the recipient is a logical thinker ensure that the order is in a logical sequence and the words are straightforward and unemotional.
4. If the communication is aimed at an individual, you can plan very specifically. If it is aimed at a group, it is not as easy to do that as you need to consider a number of preferences.
5. If you are writing to a group, it is worth investing time in considering what is the style and expectation of each recipient and ensuring that these are satisfied as much as possible.

Exercise B

Chatty – you would use this style with family and friends, or work colleagues with whom you have a good relationship.

Directional – you would use this style when you are giving instructions, e.g. to a child, giving directions, or where you are explaining a process and you want it to be carried out as instructed.

Coaching – you would use this style where you wanted to be supportive and encouraging. This is generally used to help people find the answers for themselves and is a good way to support development. This is generally a style that must be used over a long period of time.

3

Formal vs Informal – Meetings, Minutes, Actions and Follow-up

We tend to think of successful communication in business as requiring 'professionalism' and formality and yet some excellent decisions have been made in a huddle around the coffee machine. Informal and formal communications are complimentary but there is sometimes a challenge in reaching equilibrium as we tend to either be too formal or too informal.

In this chapter we will consider when formal and informal communication is most effective.

Formal

a) When is it appropriate to use formal communication?

Generally speaking, formal communication is reserved for business activity. Most organisations have a structure to their communication to allow it to flow up and down the organisation hierarchy. This is especially important where there is a strong vertical division of work.

'The brain is a wonderful organ; it starts working the moment you get up in the morning and does not stop until you get into the office.'

Robert Frost

Formality in communication says a lot about both a small business and a large corporate organisation. Communication is the way in which we create our brand and our identity. Through words and, where appropriate, associated visuals such as business cards, letter heads, marketing literature and so on, the brand becomes instantly recognisable to employees and customers alike. As we stress throughout this book, people initially buy you then your product, so the way you communicate is critical.

In many organisations, standard letters are commonplace and these reflect the corporate 'tone of voice'.

Example – Formal business communication

> RS Property Management
> Empire House
> Edinburgh Road
> Edinburgh
> EH11 6PT
>
> 26 July 2004
>
> Ms L Jones
> 12 Main Street
> Burnhouse
> West Lothian
> EH61 4NZ
>
> Dear Ms Jones
>
> PROPERTY MANAGEMENT
>
> Thank you for your enquiry regarding our management services. Please find enclosed our management package, which I am sure you will find very competitive.
> If you wish our Property Manager to visit you at the property, and this would, of course, be without cost or commitment to yourself, please do not hesitate to contact me to arrange a mutually convenient time.
> Details of our standard fees are contained within the pack.
> We trust this is of interest to you and look forward to hearing from you further. If we can be of any further assistance please do not hesitate to contact us.
>
> Yours sincerely
>
>
> Mary Brown
> Property Manager

The potential downside of formal corporate communication is that it can be peppered with lifeless words, e.g. 'key,' 'enhance', 'flexible,' 'value' etc. These words creep into both verbal and written communication and potentially detract from the listener's or reader's understanding.

By relying on a common, largely unemotional vocabulary, organisations and small businesses may miss the chance to differentiate themselves. This can limit their ability to show empathy with their customers and therefore they can potentially miss the opportunity to build relationships.

b) Why the need for formal communication?

One of the reasons for retaining good quality information is that we live in times where there is an increasing level of legislation. There are currently three pieces of legislation that we need to consider when we are communicating:

- ☑ Data Protection Act 1998
- ☑ Freedom of Information Act 2000
- ☑ Privacy and Electronic Communications Regulations 2003

This legislation seeks to protect the organisation and the individual and sets out requirements for retaining and releasing information. Full details and guidelines can be obtained from the Information Commissioner's office at **www.informationcommissioner.gov.uk**

Formal communication allows for an increase in reliability and traceability. Most importantly, it creates an accurate paper trail of what was and wasn't said.

The structure (content) of formal communication can extend to the framework (layout) of communications, as these examples show..

- When reporting on a project, formal reporting provides a structured way to build up accountability with the whole project team. A consistent report layout is put in place to ensure regular (both in terms of timing and style) reports that are submitted and circulated. Consistent communication ensures that each individual understands the required outcomes at the outset of the project.

• It can be the agreed way a committee reports to employees. This may simply be the regular circulation of a minute of a meeting. The result of this is to build an expectation of this particular method as a successful way of communication to ensure the message is not lost or missed.

 Exercise A:

List advantages and disadvantages of formal communication.

(See end of chapter for answers)

---

c) A structured approach to formal communications that works

In developing formal communication, there are a number of steps that can be followed to ensure that you are communicating effectively.

1. **Assess the current state.** Simply put, what is the current position, of what it is that you want to change, and if appropriate, do you know how your customers or employees feel about the current position? If not, it may be a good idea to ask them.

2. **Identify your communication needs.** That is, what is it that you want to change or communicate. Develop an action plan for delivery.

3. **Plan your tactics.**
   • What are the key messages?
   • What is the appropriate method of communication?
   • What is the timescale?
   • Who is responsible?

4. **Evaluate**. Have you achieved what you set out to achieve? Do you know how your customers or employees feel about the new position? If not, it may be a good idea to ask them!

Meetings

The culture of some organisations is such that a 'meeting' is required to have a conversation with someone else! This can result in there being a plethora of meetings which are unnecessarily formal and, more importantly, affect both productiveness and staff effectiveness. In short – they hit the bottom line.

Time is an extremely precious resource. To ensure that you get the most value from meetings, assess what you do against the following checklist.

? Do you know the purpose of the meeting?

? Do you always review the agenda in advance?

? Are you sure that you are the right person to attend?

? Do you check what is required of the attendees, e.g. information sharing, decision making etc?

? Do you check out the venue, timing and who else is attending? This (if they all do it!) allows everyone to arrive promptly, reducing delays in the meeting starting.

? Do you check to see if there are any papers (including previous minutes) which are to be read in advance? If there are, make sure you read them. This will allow you to contribute fully because you will be up to speed with the topic. It is also simply good manners.

? Do you give the meeting your full attention?

? Do you ask relevant questions to check your understanding?

*'Don't be afraid to ask dumb questions; they're easier
to handle than dumb mistakes.'*

Anon

? Do you support the chairperson in keeping to the agenda?

? Do you switch off your mobile phone and do not read emails during the meeting?

A special point about agendas

If there is to be a follow-up meeting, ensure that the next agenda is discussed at the end of the meeting. This allows the agenda to be shaped while the key points are fresh in the minds of the attendees. It also ensures that any additional attendees are agreed upon and given sufficient notice to allow them to attend.

The agenda is critical to the success of a meeting. Give time either to preparing the agenda if you are chairing the meeting or reading the agenda if you are an attendee. It is also good practice to circulate the agenda (along with action points from the previous meeting) at least a week in advance. This allows for adequate time to prepare and review the papers.

Example Agenda

Sales Project Meeting
5 June 2005, Lowther Room

Attending: **Apologies:**

Jim Thomson (JT) chair   Ian Black (IB)
Alison Crow (AC)   Lynn Robertson (LR)
Steve Barnett (SB)
Mike Mitchell (MM)
Susan Smith (SS)
Vicki McLaren (VM) minutes

Time	Item	Lead	Purpose	Notes
9.00 - 9.15	Review of minutes and action points	JT	Review and update	See minutes and action points from meeting on 22 May
9.15 - 9.45	Marketing materials	MM	Decision making	Review presentation and visuals
9.45 10.15	Customer feedback survey	SS	Information	Review survey - output
	10.15 - 10.30	Comfort Break		
10.30 11.50	Review of milestones and risks for each sub-project	All	Discuss	Review all - project updates
11.50 - 12.00	Agenda for next meeting	All	Discuss	
12.00	Close			

Minutes

The minute of a meeting can be invaluable – however, this depends on the nature and purpose of the meeting. There are two styles of minutes:

- **Record of the meeting and action points.** This is generally appropriate where the purpose of the meeting is decision focused. It allows for decisions and actions to be recorded.

- **Record of action points.** This is generally appropriate where fewer decisions are being made. However, through discussions, actions are identified and it is a record of who has agreed to do what and by when.

A word of caution – translating the spoken word into a written minute of a meeting can be difficult. Review the language, tone and context to ensure that they accurately reflect the discussion. This is especially true of verbatim notes. Mis-quotes or careless note taking can easily cause offence.

Is it ever appropriate not to have minutes?

'Minds are like parachutes; they work best when open.'
Lord Thomas Dewar

During informal meetings, it is usually inappropriate to take a minute of the meeting. It is however, good practice to send a note or email clarifying the agreement between the attendees.

Where there is a high degree of trust and accountability within the group, there is sometimes no need to take minutes. I work within a team where this is in place. The standards and responsibilities have been outlined and all attendees understand that they are responsible for recording their own action points and updating the team prior to the next meeting. This approach increases employee engagement and cuts down on unnecessary workload and bureaucracy.

Action points

Where action points are recorded, it is appropriate that they contain sufficient information to set out what has to be done by whom and within what timescale.

The same cautionary note applies to the noting of action points as it does to minutes. See earlier in this chapter.

Example

Action points from Sales meeting on 5 June			
Action	**Respons-ibility**	**Timescale**	**Status**
Investigate anomalies in customer survey data	SS	10 June	Com-plete
Provide team's feedback on visual materials to design company and arrange for materials to be re-circulated	MM	12 June	
Cascade details of new sales model	Sales Managers	By next meeting	

The review of the actions can be an arduous task at the start of each meeting. It is good practice to circulate them prior to the agenda being issued. This allows the status to be updated, i.e. those that have been completed to be marked as such. The completed actions need only be discussed if there is a particular query. An updated version of the actions should always be circulated with the meeting agenda.

The skill of chairing a meeting

There is a skill to chairing a meeting which requires careful and experienced communication. The role of the chairperson is to facilitate passage through the agenda, to ensure the agenda is covered and that adequate discussion and progress is made against each of the items.

There are occasions when the chairman will need to bring the meeting to order. This may be because the discussion has gone off at a tangent or because a participant is behaving inappropriately. The skill in doing this is to close down the conversation without discouraging participation later in the meeting. A way to do this is to say, *'that is a very good point that needs more detailed discussion – can we discuss outside of today's meeting.'*

There are other times where the chairman needs to encourage some of the delegates to contribute. Again there is a skill to this to ensure that the person is not embarrassed. To do this, choose a point when you know that the person is on safe ground, i.e. they know about the topic being discussed. You could say, *'Fred, you have been involved in this, what do you think?'*

> For some fascinating and radical ideas about meetings, see the companion book to this – *'Become a Meeting Anarchist in 90 Minutes'*, by Christopher Parr.

Informal

When is it appropriate to use informal communication?

All communication is about building relationships. Informal communication is the most effective way of building relationships as it is people focused.

Golden Rule 10

It is easier to make friends than enemies.

 Exercise:

Think about the ways in which you communicate informally. Write down 3 points describing your purpose and 3 points describing how you communicate with the following groups:

- your family

- your friends

- your work colleagues.

What trends do you see. What works well and what could you improve upon?

How to succeed in informal communication

Informal communication relies on getting to know the person better and allowing him or her to get to know you. The beauty of this is that it can take place anywhere; it can be a conversation in the lift, waiting in the lunch queue or it can be an email 'chat'.

> *'No one should pay attention to a man delivering a lecture or a sermon on his "philosophy of life" until he knows exactly how he treats his wife, his children, his neighbours, his friends, his subordinates and his enemies.'*
>
> Sydney Harris

✍ **Exercise: Improving informal communication**

Seek opportunities to start a conversation:

- in the lift

- in the queue at the checkout

- on the escalator.

Be observant (refer to chapter 5) - ask a relevant question.

- Do you work in x department?

- Have you tried y - would you recommend them?

- What do you think of the ladies' department in this shop?

Initially, this may seem quite unnatural but with practice you will soon enjoy the art of conversation.

Structure of informal communication

Informal communication is less structured than formal communication. It is less planned, and rather spontaneous and is generally shorter. It is usually between two people or a small group of people.

It is more important to be aware of others in informal communication than it is in formal communication. This includes awareness of your own and others' body language – which was mentioned in chapter 1.

It is also helpful to be aware of auditory signals. The proverb says, *'The eyes are the window to the soul'* but the voice can give an equally good insight. People can work on their smile and because of an increase in plastic surgery, people can now buy their look! But voices are genuine. You can tell if the person is comfortable with you, not putting up barriers. When someone's voice is flat or quiet, you don't have any idea what they are feeling or thinking.

✐ **Exercise: Improving informal communication**

When you are next in a place full of strangers, say, on a train journey, close your eyes for a few minutes and listen to one person speaking.

Ignore the words - what is her voice saying?

- Is there warmth?

- Genuine enthusiasm?

- Sincerity?

- Does she express herself in a way that is real or is she trying too hard?

- Is she comfortable with herself?

- Does she vary her pace and tone of voice?

- Is she present and interested in the conversation?

Influencing through informal communication

Informal communication can be used effectively to influence in a formal setting. The most important rule is to be yourself and allow others to be themselves. Be respectful of different opinions and points of view.

There are three ways to influence through informal communication:

1 **Find a champion**. That is someone who shares your passion and enthusiasm and is willing to share his or her views. This person is likely to echo, support and agree with your ideas in a formal setting. Especially if you have taken the opportunity to share these thoughts and ideas in advance.

2 Use informal conversations and meetings to **gather feedback** and views. For example, if you are preparing a report, take time to share the paper with all of the interested parties before it is presented. Gather and amend in light of their feedback. This may

appear time consuming and bureaucratic but the investment will allow you to gather ideas and gain support to ensure that once the report is presented, it is more likely to be supported.

3   **Establish supporters**. Quite simply build good relationships with people to ensure that they will support you and be constructive in sharing their views and feedback.

Networking

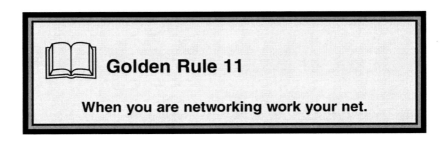

appear

When you are networking work your net.

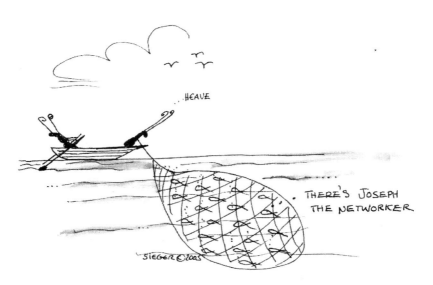

54

Susan Baxter, MD of Expandingbusiness Ltd, was keen to expand her company, but needed investment of £30k to implement her business plan.

Her bank started out by being supportive but became less so over time. *'They were asking for extra security that I didn't think was necessary,'* explained Susan.

She attended a networking event and bumped into a bank manager from another bank. He invited her to come and talk to him about her requirements. The result was that the old bank became history. The loan was granted by the new bank and Susan is now getting a much better service. *'Much better than just walking in off the street,'* she said.

Networking is a common activity associated with business but because of the fear of embarrassment, e.g. I may make a fool of myself, it is not recognised as a relationship-building tool outside work. Networking is simply an activity aimed at:

- ✓ expanding your list of contacts – for example, this can be to build relationships to get sales, to meet people across the organisation you work for, expand your circle of friends and so on

- ✓ building relations

- ✓ improving your or your company's visibility

- ✓ obtaining information

- ✓ sharing experiences

- ✓ stimulating ideas.

Networking is a speculative activity. No matter how much you plan, you can never be sure which phone call, event or conversation will lead you to the place you want to be. It can however be an extremely rewarding and satisfying activity.

Golden Rule 12

Use networking to grow your circle of contacts and friends.

Planning

Meeting people for the first time can be emotionally taxing. See the exercise earlier in the chapter about how to improve informal communication; this will help you feel more comfortable in talking to people you do not know.

- Choosing the right activity or event is key. It is key that you make sure that the people you wish to meet are likely to attend the same event. For example, if you are an HR Manager, it is highly likely that you will meet like-minded individuals at a Chartered Institute of Personnel and Development Event.

- Don't miss the opportunity to contact individuals directly. When I was looking for a new job, I made a list of companies that I would like to work for and made a list of key contacts. I then phoned them and asked for a meeting. Although a daunting task, I was very pleasantly surprised that the vast majority agreed to meet with me. In fact, it is as a result of this that I got my current job.

✍ **Exercise: Network plan**

Make a list:

1. Who do you want to meet?

2. Where are you likely to meet them?

3. Why do you want to meet them?

4. When are you likely to meet them?

5. What would you say when you meet them?

- If you are attending an event, get the guest list in advance or ask the host who will be attending. This gives you the opportunity to see who is attending, establish who you would like to meet and potentially find out a little bit about them. If it is a dinner, you could ask the host or organiser to seat you next to the person you would most like to meet.

- Walking into a room full of strangers can be extremely nerve-racking even for the most experienced networker.

  - Scan the room for friendly faces – I often do this while I am getting myself a drink.

  - Seek out people who are standing on their own or a larger group of people. Be aware that a group of two people may be having a personal or confidential conversation.

  - Make your introduction.

Example introduction

Hi, I am June Black from XYZ Associates - do you mind if I join you?

- Prepare a short verbal CV for yourself. For business, this should include a description of your role and your company and what you find especially interesting or enjoyable. For personal, this should contain a bit about you, where you live, your interests and hobbies. It is a good idea to rehearse these so that they flow naturally and easily when you are asked to describe yourself. Try to keep this to less than two minutes.

✎ Exercise:

In no more than 100 words write two CVs, one business and one personal. Read these back and record them. Do you sound interesting. How long did you take?

- When introduced to someone, try to remember his or her name. Make an effort to repeat the name back during the conversation. This helps to commit it to your memory. However, do this sparingly as it can start to sound false.

- Ask questions to find common ground. Show interest in what is being said and share experiences.

- Eye contact and body language are important – see Chapter 1. It is equally important to be alert to the body language of the other person, to read their signals to you and respond accordingly.

- It is important to move on to allow you and the other person to meet other people. This can be done by making an excuse to go for another drink or go to the toilet, or by saying, 'I see xxx over there – I really want to speak to him, will you excuse me.'

● Where appropriate, ask people you have met for their business card or contact details. You should only do this where you genuinely want to follow up with them.

Retaining information

I always keep business cards. It is amazing how often I have phoned someone years after I have met them, even if it only to ask them to introduce me to someone else.

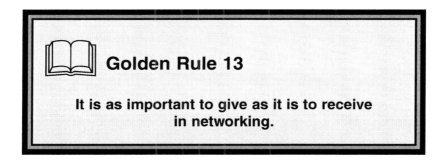

Golden Rule 13

It is as important to give as it is to receive in networking.

If you have said that you will contact someone after a first meeting, do so. It is always good practice to send a note or email saying how much you enjoyed meeting them. Even better, is to follow up with a phone call. This is the best way to allow your personality to show through. These actions will increase the likelihood of being remembered by others.

Likewise, if someone has asked to contact you and they are seeking information, support or advice, try to be as helpful as possible. Remember, networking is about growing your circle of contacts and you never know when you may require their help.

Formal and informal communications are complimentary

Formal and informal communications compliment each other and we should always seek a mixture of both. Think about how you deal with people at work; it is always easier to deal with people once you have met them, rather than those that you have to deal with remotely.

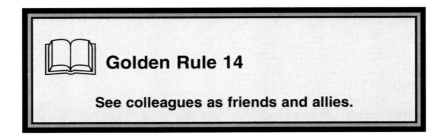

Golden Rule 14

See colleagues as friends and allies.

Some practical hints and tips

✓ Always get to meetings five minutes ahead of their start time. This allows you the opportunity of chatting to other attendees and getting to know them.

✓ Be open and honest in all of your communication whether written or spoken. Give an insight to your interests and let your personality shine through.

✓ When you are trying to influence, it is helpful to collect feedback and views informally prior to presenting your position. This ensures engagement, i.e. no surprises, and minimises potential resistance as people feel involved in shaping the outcome.

✓ **Network, network, network**. The more people you get to know, the better. You will have more fun and achieve more.

Golden Rule 15

Relationships are the key to happiness and success.

Chapter 3 – Exercise answer page

Exercise A:

Advantages: It focuses on the key points and it is less likely that these will be lost in over-familiarity. It is more structured and there is therefore there is greater clarity. It is generally formally recorded by way of minutes, action points etc and is therefore traceable.

Disadvantages: it can limit relationship building because there is limited personal interaction between the individuals. May create lack of trust because documents are retained for future reference.

'When all men think alike, no one thinks very much.'
Walter Lippmann

4

Emails, Voicemails and Papertrails

The internet came into existence in the mid to late 1970s. Since then there has been explosive growth in communication technology. We now live in an age where both in and out of work, we are dependant upon an array of communication gadgets which are rapidly becoming an essential part of our everyday lives. There are many advantages to the internet, but who would have thought that many of us would now be ordering our groceries via the web. This technology has also increased price competition and offered an alternative and cheaper delivery channel. Travel, for example, is cheaper than before and booking arrangements are more self-service.

The downside of the internet is that along with security issues (sadly it has supported an increase in some criminal activity, e.g. it has increased accessibility to child pornography), users often say they miss talking directly to someone on the end of the phone. Our transactions and communications have become anonymous.

Along with the growth in the internet, email too has become much more commonplace. Email was meant to make our lives easier but many employees end up feeling stressed by their inbox. Email is now a feature of modern life. We live in a time when communication is fast and relentless and where email, when used appropriately, has become an extremely powerful tool.

✑ **Exercise:**

Pause for a moment and think about how you rely upon the internet and email outside work.

According to a recent survey, 75% of firms now acknowledge that email is critical to their business. It is, however one that has been and continues to be abused to the extent that the Chartered Institute of Personnel and Development are predicting that there will shortly be a surge of claims of work-related stress caused by the volume of email traffic. The fact that email stress is now accounting for a growing percentage of sick leave was confirmed in a survey by Veritas Software. They not only confirmed email as a major catalyst for workplace stress but also found that dependency has become so great that 30 minutes without access causes two thirds of us to become irritated. Just think about how you felt the last time your PC crashed or the server went down and vital unsaved information was lost!

Email – a communication tool

Email can be an extremely effective communication tool. It has nearly the immediacy of conversation. The downsides are that it is completely devoid of body language and because of the fast pace, we generally take less care in constructing messages than we would if it was a letter or memo. There is also the expectation (or forlorn hope) of an immediate reply.

The improvement in wireless technology has resulted in an increase in accessibility of email. You can access emails from hotels, cafes, trains and even some supermarkets using laptops or one of the growing number of hand-held devices such as Blackberrys. This is certainly driving a change in behaviour and is muddying the line between work and life.

Using email effectively to achieve a work life balance

 Golden Rule 16

Take control of your electronic communication before it takes control of you.

'We are not retreating. We are advancing in another direction.'
Douglas MacArthur

Dr Monica Seeley, Fellow of the Imperial College Business School, suggests that we waste up to 16 days per year dealing with unwanted emails. Many of us have become slaves to email. We feel compelled to respond to the 'ping' every time a new message enters our in box. This can make us unproductive as we do not give our attention to the activities we have prioritised. It is now not uncommon in some organisations to find that email has replaced conversations. The explanation given is that it does not interrupt the receiver while they are concentrating on another activity.

There are a few simple tips to help manage email traffic:

✓ **Set aside specific times of the day** to review your inbox. It is recommended that this is limited to 30 minute chunks. Good time management practice is to prioritise your workload at the end of each day for the following day. You therefore may wish to consider reviewing your messages just before you start your planning activity. This allows you to factor in any activities that may need to be done urgently.

✓ **Challenge the behaviours of others**. Our inability to cope with emails is, to a large extent, caused by email abuse. This comes in various forms:
  a) inappropriate copying in of messages
  b) messages which just acknowledge receipt
  c) messages which expect a response in an inappropriate timescale.

✓ Set your own **standards** to work to and ask those people emailing you to respect and abide by your standards. You may even encourage others to follow your example.

  a) It is the easiest thing in the world to build a distribution list, to ensure that everyone who may have an interest is copied in. If you receive a message that is not relevant; pick up the phone or go and speak to the person who has sent it. A little investment will result in a reduction of inappropriate messages. It is worth explaining that you wish to manage your email effectively and ask them why they copied you into the email.

  b) Similarly, messages which just acknowledge receipt are not useful and serve only to increase email volume. Pick up the phone or go and speak to the person who has sent it. Politely explain to them that if you required a receipt you would have 'flagged' the message

  c) The instant nature of email often means that there is an expectation of an instant response. This should be treated in the same way as other work and be prioritised. However, you should seek to explain your timescales to the emailer in the same way you would with any other piece of work. It is good practice to insert the timescale of the required response in the subject header,

Make a clear divide, what ever is appropriate for you, between work and the rest of your life and try to stick to that. This creates an understanding and manages the expectations of others.

Depending upon the culture of your organisation, challenging in this way can be a little daunting. You can, however, be sure that others will wish to improve email effectiveness and you may wish to consider agreeing some 'challenging' behaviours that will be adopted across your whole team.

Remember – to improve the effectiveness of email, you have to practice what you preach!

 Exercise:

Make an action plan to improve the way that you manage your email.

Email etiquette

Golden Rule 17

Do to others what you'd like them to do to you email-wise.

Email is simply another form of communication and is most effective when it is planned and considered in that way. The following are some tips to consider when using email:

● First consider if email is an appropriate medium for the type of communication you have in mind. Would it be better expressed in a letter or phone call?

● Use email the way you would like it used and lead by example.
  • Use meaningful subject headings.
  • Use priority status and flags sparingly and only when required.
  • It you require a response within a particular timescale insert this into the heading.

● Take another look before you send a message. It is helpful to put yourself in the shoes of your audience and consider how they will read the message. This is required especially if you are complaining or are angry.

'When you're angry always count to ten before saying anything. It'll give you more time to come up with the right insult.'

● Reply effectively. It may seem obvious but ensure it is clear that you are responding to something specific either by including the previous email chain or by putting the subject in context in a new message.

● Refer back to Chapter 2, Purpose of communication – 'How to influence rather than make a noise' to see hints and tips on content. Use appropriate language. It is important to get your message clearly understood. Think about the context, the message and most importantly your recipient.

'Humour is the great thing, the saving thing. The minute it crops up, all our irritations and resentments slip away, and a sunny spirit takes their place.'
Mark Twain

Email is a very effective informal method of communication and humour can be used effectively Do use it only where it will not be misinterpreted or cause offence.

- Use text, font and colour appropriately. It is helpful to keep in mind that email is another method of communication. Bizarre typefaces can detract from understanding the message. It is also worth remembering that writing in capital letters indicates that you are shouting and therefore should be used sparingly.

- Avoid sending documents that are in fancy or unusual formats. This can lead to frustration if the recipient is then unable to open and read them.

- Use a signature at the end of emails. This should be limited to just a few lines and contain your key contact details.

Example of a simple signature bar for emails

John Brown, Operations Manager, XYZ Co Ltd,   jbrown@xyzcl.com
15 The Road, Anytown, BB22 CC33
Telephone: 01234 567890   Mobile: 0727 272727

- Avoid using 'smileys' and other graphics unless you know the person well. I was sent an email that should have been a private reply to someone's job application. Worse, than that, it was sent to four other recipients! All now knew who was in contention for the post. It was blithely signed by 'Bob' with two 'smileys' clinking beer glasses. I don't think any of the recipients felt like drinking beer with Bob – or his boss would when he found out!

- Check if it is okay to send large attachments. It is frustrating if an incoming email takes up the PC's memory capacity.

 Exercise:

1. Review your email templates and make sure that they are set up using the hints and tips above.

2. Review your last 10 'sent' emails. Would they be different if you were sending them now? List your lessons learned.

Retaining information

Email is a highly effective way of retaining information. The challenge is often how to retrieve it effectively. It is relatively simple to structure your mailbox into folders and sub-folders to keep messages well organised. I also colour code high priority messages to allow me to see them easily.

Example

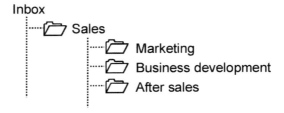

Voicemail and text messaging as communication tools

With the advancement and increase in the numbers of mobile phones, the use of voicemail is increasing.

Voicemail is often overlooked as a communication tool and many people avoid leaving messages because they want a personal response, or they just simply get embarrassed. Used effectively, voicemail can be a good way to communicate your brand or win a meeting as it allows your personality to come over in the message.

In leaving a voicemail message, you should give:

- your name
- your company
- the date and time
- a contact number
- a brief message.

Example

Hi, James, this is Susan Walsh from International Co, on 25 July at 3pm. Would you please call me on 01745 112233 to discuss some modifications to our contract. Thank you.

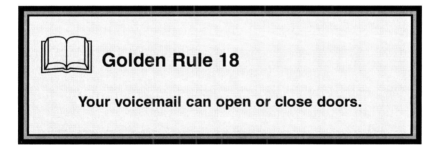

Golden Rule 18

Your voicemail can open or close doors.

When preparing to make a telephone call, plan in the same way you would for any other conversation:

- Know why you are entering the conversation.

  - *social* – much less formal, relaxed and easier to go with the flow
  - *business* – increased need to make an impression especially if this is the first time you have spoken to the person. You want your message to be clear and articulate. Consider the purpose (the beginning), the three key messages (the middle) and what action action you want the listener to undertake (the end).

● The tone, pace and pitch of your voice tells the listener a lot about you. They can hear if you are trying too hard, therefore it is important to be yourself, be genuine and show that you are interested in what you are saying.

  • Use the listener's name, this is especially powerful at the start and end of the message.
  • Smile – this comes through in your voice.
  • Breathe – this will ensure your pace is not too rushed.
  • In a voice message, the aim is to engage the listener sufficiently to encourage them to call you back. It is good practice to aim to talk for no more than one minute.

✐ **Exercise:**

In no more than 50 words, write out an advert selling yourself. Record it as a message.

What do you hear, what is your first impression, would you buy from this person?

Retaining information

In business, it is essential that you know what you have said, when you said it and to whom. Setting up and maintaining a simple contact database can help with this.

Example

Contact database

Name	Date of	Content	Action	Follow up
Fred Smith	1 June	Message left	Call back	3 June
Ann Black	1 June	Gave overview of service	Send literature	14 June
Steve Jones	1 June	Gave overview of service	Meeting arranged	20 June

Text Messaging

Text messaging is becoming increasingly popular especially with young people as it is generally cheaper than making a mobile phone call. It is a hybrid between email and voice messaging. It can be used effectively in business but only for short messages, and, where the audience is receptive to it, e.g. acknowledging graduate recruitment applications. The informality can sometimes mean that we do not maintain good records for follow up so text messaging should be limited to non-business communication or where there is no real need to retain a record of the contact.

5

How to Give Business Situations the Personal Touch

In the introduction to this book, we mentioned the results of Marcus Buckingham and Donald Clifton's latest Gallup Organisation meta-analysis which showed that globally, only 20% of employees felt that their strengths were used at work, and a staggering 83% were at work but not engaged. However, if we look at individuals, small businesses and larger corporations that have high engagement with clients and staff, there is one thing they have in common. They have a personal touch in communication style which, by making those they work with feel *significant*, automatically ensures constructive dialogue, trust, engagement, better work/life balance, a positive approach to challenges, increased client base, healthier profits and more. A key part of excellent communications is to use business situations as a way of winning the hearts and minds of staff, clients and potential clients – in short that they, and you, feel appreciated.

One of the other exciting spin-offs of this type of communication style is that we will build networks of contacts. An excellent book on this is *'The Tipping Point'* by Malcolm Gladwell.

Before we look at the personal touch in communication, perhaps a key question we need to ask is how often do you meet with staff or business contacts on a one-to-one basis and how do you approach that session? Our research has found that with individuals or organisations that hold 'process-only' one-to-ones with staff, i.e. facts, figures, targets and performance, the Gallup Survey figures of dis-engaged staff were confirmed. Other individuals and organisations that approached one-to-ones as an opportunity to let people talk about their personal situations, such as difficulty finding child-minders, financial worries or whatever, had far better engagement and improved performance. One team leader, who suffered from poor health herself, had a team that won a national award for teamwork and outstanding performance. When I asked her what she did, she said she simply had short weekly one-to-ones with team members and got to know them. One team member who had a record of absenteeism became one of the best performers. Why? Simply because her team leader had talked with her, listened and made helpful affirming suggestions, this person felt as if she mattered – and that gave her a great reason for getting out of bed and going to work.

'Good management is the art of making problems so interesting and their solutions so constructive that everyone wants to get to work and deal with them.'

Paul Hawken

✎ **Exercise:**

Think of some of your business clients - what percentage of time is used on possible business opportunities and what percentage on getting to know the other person?

Think of your staff or team members - do you have a consistent and gracious approach to getting to know them?

Let us be clear at this stage that when we talk about the personal touch in communication, we are not talking 'touchy-feely', trampling boundaries or changing your personality! There are some simple communication tools that are very effective and enhance your position as an influencer and win you relationships.

We're going to run through various scenarios you will have found yourself in and look at what works and what doesn't work in each one.

Scenario 1 – Maximising meetings and interviews

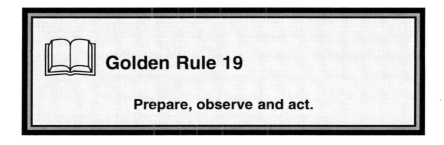

Golden Rule 19

Prepare, observe and act.

We hold meetings and interviews to learn and share information and make decisions that will create movement and growth for business. We want to ensure that our thoughts are communicated in such a way that we get the outcomes needed for our business or organisation. This is why the personal touch is so important and Golden Rule 20 is the key.

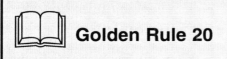

Golden Rule 20

The personal touch is the only way to touch the person - i.e. people buy you, not the product.

a) Prepare – questions you need to ask yourself

- Who will be at the meeting/interview?
- What are their names, positions?
- What background information do you have?

Personal touch that works: introducing yourself with a smile, warmly shaking hands and using the other person's name and referring to something you have learned from your preparation. For example, *'Pleased to meet you, John. I understand your office is near the golf course. Are you a keen golfer yourself?'* Nowadays, most people introduce themselves using first names and the best thing is to respond in kind where appropriate.

Personal touch that doesn't work: meetings and interviews tend to be held in a variety of venues ranging from board rooms to Starbucks – we've covered this in Chapter 3, but some reminders are:

- ☒ beware slipping into over-familiarity just because the venue is informal!

- ☒ Beware of overuse of first names as it comes across as forgetful (poor at remembering names so have to repeat them to retain them), over-familiar ('we really are almost friends even though we've only met'), or desperate to be noticed!

b) Observe and act

A key element in communication is observation – if you notice what is going on around you, it is easier to link that to a good conversation opener or, if there is a distinct 'stuckness', to find a way to restart the conversation. Good observation allows you to take the initiative in a variety of ways that all help as vehicles for creating conversation. This is especially useful if you don't know the other people and are wondering how to ease into conversation.

- Observe: What is the room/venue like, e.g. hot, cold, airy, dingy
- Act: Possibly open a window, turn up the heating etc

Creative conversation opener: *'I'm finding it quite hot in here. Do you mind if I open a window? What kind of climate do you like best for holidays/are you a hot or cold weather person etc ...?*

- Observe: What are the people/person like, e.g. wearing a smart suit, good colours, looking healthy, tired etc
- Act: Approach people and introduce yourself

Creative conversation opener: General opener – *'I don't think we've met – I'm Jo Smith. Are you with Bloggs the Builders (or whatever)?*
Specific opener, e.g. if they look tired – *'I don't think we've met – I'm Jo Smith. I don't know about you, but I feel a little tired with this heat/long morning. There are a couple of chairs free over by the window – would you like to have coffee over there?'*

- Observe: The coffee on the table is not within reach of everyone
- Act: Is there someone you can offer to serve?

✎ **Exercise:** Observations leading to conversations

Every time you look at something, see if you can create a conversation link from it.

For example: A coffee cup on a desk - could create the following:

- Can I take your cup for you, by the way I'm ...

- I'm just on my way to get some coffee, can I get you some? By the way, I really liked your idea for the new marketing programme - why don't we discuss it later.

You might be thinking this kind of conversational gambit is not so relevant to interviews but they are. Why? Because if you come across as relaxed and confident, even if you are not the right person for the job, you will have made a great impression and, most importantly, people will talk positively about you to others. Who knows where that will lead!

Scenario 2 – Staff appraisals

When it comes to staff appraisals or annual job evaluations, there is a sense of nervous anticipation for both the person delivering the findings and the person receiving the good or not so good news. One of the first questions you have to ask yourself is: 'Am I a person-centred person or a self-centred person?' This is really important as it will affect the way you use your personality and how you speak. Are you easy to work with or are you a bully? Are you sensitive to other people's needs and emotions or are you egotistical? Are you so aware of how you feel that you can't hear what other people are trying to explain to you?

I have been saddened and irritated to hear people boasting about how they 'roasted' a member of staff at their appraisal. Aggressive and negative speech is normative in many organisations and the result is a fear culture. In one company, it was expected that new staff would only last three years then have burnout, and what was worse, nobody thought there was anything wrong with that!

It is the part of a good shepherd to shear his flock, not to skin it.
Latin proverb

Words of wisdom for the appraiser – always remember you are dealing with a person who has feelings, emotions, dreams, friends and family.

Words of wisdom for the appraisee – always remember you are dealing with a person who has feelings, emotions, dreams, friends and family!

In the Chapter on dealing with difficult people, we'll look at how to deal with individuals who are bullies, whether in management, on the shop floor or business contacts.

The appraiser

People coming for their annual review, which may involve a bonus or not as the case may be, can come in various states of mind. For example:

* I'm looking forward to this as I think I've done really well (when in fact they haven't)
* I'm not looking forward to this as I've been dodging work and don't get on with my colleagues (which is true)
* I really need this bonus to help pay off my debts/holiday/ whatever
* Having chatted with my boss throughout the year, this will just confirm how well things are going and, I may be up for promotion.

The dynamics of the session will be affected by whatever the individual's mindset is. If there is something he or she needs to be told, whether good news or not, if you or the appraisee have come to the meeting with an unrealistic picture of what is going to happen, certain things can result from this. There can be: misunderstanding, defensive arguing, lack of really hearing what is being said and at some point, emotions will be stirred. As the appraiser, there are some easy communication tips that can create just the environment you need for a successful meeting – even ones that include bad news!

 Golden Rule 21

The way you treat your people is the model they will adopt for treating others.

Firstly we'll look at the meetings that involve good news and healthy discussion.

1. Scene setting – for happy appraisals

☑ Well before the appraisal meeting, drop by the person's desk/office and say how much you're looking forward to the appraisal session. If he is not geographically close, send a warm email. He will at that point understand the meeting is going to go well and will be relaxed. Even if you are busy or tired on the day, greet him with a smile. We've seen really wonderful news flattened because the deliverer was too tired to be enthusiastic.

☑ Be clear about the format of the session – when good news is being shared, sometimes important information about the next piece of work is lost. What do you want this person to go away with – is there something he needs to action?

☑ Allow time for going through the appraisal and having time to chat. This will be more productive than squashing the appraisal into too short a time slot and rushing the person out because of the next meeting. If you've delivered a great appraisal 'experience', that will be an affirming memory for both you and the appraisee for the next time.

☑ Think about the person you are meeting – how well do you know him at a personal level? Do you know what type of person he is, e.g. shy, extrovert etc. Base the language you use around his personality type.

☑ Give credit where and when it is due, even if the person who has done well is someone you don't like! 'Excellent piece of work', 'consistent high standards', 'You've really set an example to the rest of the team' are just a few examples.

2. Scene setting – for unhappy appraisals

We don't need to go into allowing time for the session, giving credit where due or basing language around the personality type but we'd like to highlight a couple of things.

☑ Well before the meeting, go see her, or call if more appropriate. If you know it's going to be difficult and you know she knows, you might simply say, 'It's been a challenging year but I'm looking forward to seeing what solutions we can come up with for next year.' Simply using the phrase 'I'm looking forward' will flag up that it will be less painful and certainly more constructive than she expects.

☑ Again, think about the format of the session and put her at her ease right from the start. Simply getting coffee, smiling and saying something like, 'I'm really pleased with some of the work you've been doing and whilst there are a couple of areas to look at, overall this hasn't been too bad a year', can set the scene for a positive result.

☑ If you are dealing with someone who is a real slacker and only scrapes by each year the book *'FISH'* by Stephen C Lundin, John Christensen and Harry Paul would be useful to read!

The appraisee

So let's look at how to respond in the next three situations:

1. You've done your best but your performance is poor

➤ Before the meeting, flag up with your boss that you're looking forward to getting insights into how to take things to the next level in the coming year.

➢ Be prepared with self-knowledge – if the poor performance was laziness, identify the specific areas and start improving your performance before the meeting. If the reason was you are in the wrong job, start looking around or ask your boss if you can move internally. Also read *'Now Discover Your Strengths'* by Marcus Buckingham and do the on-line test, or work through *'The Class Act Book'* by Mike Pegg and complete the self-discovery exercises there.

➢ It was market forces – be honest, your boss is in the same boat. Go to the appraisal with a couple of strategic suggestions.

➢ Have relaxed and engaged body language – it flags up you are keen to be a team player to help move the company forward.

2. You've had a great year and done better than expected

➢ Give praise where it is due – other staff, your boss for encouraging you, company ethos etc

➢ Enjoy being affirmed. One thing to mention is that if you have an unpleasant boss who has to have praise dragged out from between his lips, take pleasure in encouraging him to expand. For example if you've hit new targets and all you get is 'Well it's not been a bad year', you could simply ask: 'Does that mean it wasn't a good year?' or, 'How do the figures compare to last year?' ... 'Oh, they're 80% up, sounds fantastic to me!'

Golden Rule 22

Avoid being a 'lemon-sucker' - it makes your words wrinkled and sour!

3. You've not done well and you know why

If you know why, and you haven't improved it or changed your attitude, then either face up to the kind of person you are and change your attitude or, leave the organisation. There is nothing worse than hearing someone who has a list of excuses longer than the Eiffel Tower. Negative minds and negative words just sap the energy of the people who hear them and especially the person who speaks them. Eventually the 'real you' is lost in the adopted persona of negativity – just look at Gollum in Lord of the Rings!

Scenario 3 – Events and away-days

These are great opportunities to dress down, chill out, learn things in a relaxing way and get to know other people. The key to the success of this kind of event is the detail that goes into planning them. A great events organiser is worth his or her weight in gold and someone like Morag Brownlie of 1-2-1 Events, who is creative, thorough, excellent in standards and, great fun, will help achieve all the outcomes you are looking for. See **www.1-2-1events.com**. When the external context is right, the internal communications will follow.

Scenario 4 – Birthdays, anniversaries and celebrations

Bearing in mind what we said at the beginning about feeling valued and significant, birthdays, anniversaries and celebrations are a great vehicle for affirming people. You don't have to do a lot to make people feel affirmed. A post-it note on a computer screen with 'Hi Elaine, Happy Birthday – J', a card on their desk, bringing them coffee and a muffin with a candle stuck in it are simple and effective ways of giving people a great day. Some practical tips:

☑ Keep a diary of significant dates (or if you're in a large business ensure someone takes responsibility for this, e.g. HR).

☑ Keep a stock of cards for various occasions so that if you only remember on the day, you will have something to hand.

☑ Never leave anyone out – even the people you don't like.

 Golden Rule 23

If you make the world a nicer place to live in, you'll enjoy living in it too!

6

The Effects of Contagious Communication

When we talk about contagious communication, remember what we said back in the Introduction to this book that *people buy us not the product* and the experience they have through meetings, phone calls and so on all help them make up their minds. Starbucks and IKEA amongst others have understood that by creating a brand image based on experience – sofas, bespoke coffees, or little paths you can follow from one department to another – wins repeat business.

How can an individual or an organisation measure how excellent their communications 'experience' is? It is very simple – how well do their customers relate to them and refer business to them. The challenge to creating the fabulous communication 'experience' we are talking about is that there can seem to be a lot of negative people around. I'm not referring to those giving open constructive criticism but those fault-finding and doomsday scenario people who are members of the Lemon-Suckers Club. Obviously if you're reading this book you won't be one of them! How do you spot them? They come across in a couple of ways. Either spotted giving quiet asides in the loo and definitely behind backs, or sometimes quite openly at meetings or one-to-ones. There are the plain old gossips who delight in making comments about other people at a personal level and the doom-mongers who can't come up with any positive business solutions but are brilliant at knocking everyone else's! Can you identify which of the following fall into which category?

☹ 'Well, we tried that before and it never worked.'

☹ 'Joe's really frustrated about the way he's being pushed around – Andy and Sarah feel the same.'

☹ 'Of course, if she/he wears that kind of hairstyle/tie, it says a lot about their lack of taste – no wonder they can't get their team around them.'

☹ 'You've only been around a few weeks and don't understand the culture.'

☹ A couple of people talking softly, looking embarrassed when the topic of their discussion walks in, then big smiles to cover up.

It is never a problem to discuss anything but if you imagine the person you were talking about were standing listening, would you say it in a kinder or more constructive way?

> *'Let the words I say today be soft and tender*
> *for tomorrow I may have to eat them.'*
>
> Unknown

 Golden Rule 24

When being honest it is always better to sound like a flute player than a drummer.

Remember that 95% of all business comes by word of mouth referral. If we – and our staff – are talking well (regular and positive communication) to one another, then our customers will pick that up. There is nothing more infectious than someone else's enthusiasm for something, and, like every good infection, it is contagious!

a) Setting standards of communication – starting with yourself

Whether in business for yourself or working for a larger company there need to be clear standards on what is acceptable or not as a communication style. These standards are basically essential interpersonal skills that, when applied consistently, will have a knock-on effect with both customers and staff.

For businesses with more than one employee, no matter how large, the key in setting standards of communication is that everyone knows what is expected of them. You can put key words or quotes that encapsulate what you are aiming for on noticeboards, on post-it notes and so on, to remind yourself and staff of what is expected of them. The best way of course is to model best practice yourself – don't worry if you stand out or feel slightly uncomfortable!

> *'Never go to a doctor whose office plants have died.'*
> Erma Bombeck

Look at the list of key questions below – how are you in these areas?

● **Attitude** – 'Out of the abundance of your heart your mouth speaks.'

Do you have a positive approach to people in general? Are you someone who expects good things in people? When you meet people are you actively engaged in getting to know what they are thinking?

✍ **Exercise:**

- Think of conversations you have enjoyed and have left a positive impression. Write a list of the reasons for that.

- Think of conversations that have left a negative impression. Write down the reasons for that.

- What one thing could you change in the way you communicate to make talking with you a more positive experience for others?

● **Kind words and positive phrases**

Most of us will at some time have watched some of the 'fly-on-the-wall' documentaries where people are trying to sort out dysfunctional relationships at home, at work, on holiday, or Big Brother type programmes where the person left at the end is the winner. At the start, everyone does their best to come across as an adult but inevitably as tension builds, their vocabulary changes to undermine the viewers' opinion of the person they're talking about. They want to show themselves in a better light than their competitors. This happens in business too. Make a decision to use words that describe a situation rather than denigrate a person. Use phrases that are truthful but positive so that information can be passed without undermining someone's self-esteem.

✐ Exercise A:

Replace the following phrases with positive alternatives:

- You're under-performing.

- You can't do that.

- You don't seem to be getting along well with the rest of your team.

Think of other phrases that you use quite commonly but which could be better said in a more positive way.

(See end of chapter for answers)

● Ban aggressive and provocative language

We have been saddened and annoyed to hear people boasting about how they 'roasted' a member of staff or 'I really gave them a piece of my mind'. Aggressive and negative speech is normative in many organisations and the result is a fear and suspicion culture – which affects the bottom line. Unlike learning to rephrase words in a positive way, aggressive and provocative language needs to be banned immediately. It has been proven that for every one negative statement that is made, it takes ten positive ones to repair the psychological damage.

 Golden Rule 25

He who speaks acid words will eventually burn his tongue.

● **Clarity of understanding**

The hills are alive with the sound of targets

Going back to that great definition of communication as not a meeting of words but a meeting of meaning, it is always wiser to ask a question to clarify what is being meant. For example, two people can have been at the same meeting and afterwards one of them might comment on what a tiring meeting it had been. In her mind's eye, she is thinking of how hot the room had been, how she hadn't quite recovered from playing two rounds of golf the day before – or whatever. The other replies that she too had found it tiring but she is thinking of the overdosed powerpoint, endless discussions over irrelevant details and how mentally taxing it had been. If at that point, the second person then comments on how boring the powerpoint was, the first person won't necessarily agree and the first person will feel they've had conflicting messages – I found the meeting tiring but I didn't find the meeting tiring. It's always useful to ask a question that allows the person to elaborate on what he or she meant before you jump in with your views. A simple 'in what way did you find it tiring?' would have clarified everything and left the door open for a more strategic conversation.

b) Selling a communication experience – your staff

Bearing in mind all the things mentioned in the previous section, can you think of every opportunity that you have to communicate with your staff (if you haven't any staff, think of friends and family!)?. Do you notice the people who come across your path and give them your full attention, even if it's only for the few seconds when you are passing by. Do you smile? Do you remember their names – are you aware of birthdays and anniversaries? These are great opportunities to build trust and good relationships with people.

In the film *'What Women Want'* Mel Gibson ends up with the ability to hear what women are thinking and he makes full manipulative use of this. One day he 'hears' a downtrodden member of staff being very negative about herself and later, planning to take her own life. Shocked into action and challenged about his hedonistic lifestyle, he puts her needs ahead of his ambition and saves the situation and her life.

Never assume you know what is going on in someone else's life – by celebrating birthdays or whatever, it gives the opportunity to talk with people and to get to know them better. They will feel affirmed and noticed – and that will have a positive effect on you too!

c) Selling a communication experience – the customer

What do customers want? To be understood and to understand. What does this mean in practice? We've looked at setting the kinds of standards of communication which are key to creating contagious communication. Now we need to look at how to create a great communication experience for your customers (or potential clients).

● **Be clear on the brand message that is to be communicated**

By this we mean a short, succinct mission statement or 'elevator pitch' (as much information as you can come out with to a stranger, in a short floor-to-floor elevator ride). One of the best examples of this is Fuji films whose main competitor was Kodak. During a brainstorming session, Fuji staff were trying to come up with a mission statement that would reflect the fact that they were as good and in fact, even better, than Kodak. After a while, one bright person came up with the simple mission statement: Kill Kodak – and that is what Fuji set out to do by famously flying a balloon over Kodak's headquarters for a year. The resulting publicity did the rest!

Most companies' mission statements require a reader with a long attention span and the ability to carry several concepts at the same time. Keep your brand message simple and effective. In terms of elevator pitch, the same applies but also bear the following in mind. When you say what you do, or represent, be careful that you won't be stereotyped. For example, if you are an accountant, the moment you say what you do, the people listening will decide whether they want to know more based on their own experience of accountants. If that's negative, you're stymied. If it's positive that's not so bad.

Robin Sieger, a fantastic motivational speaker, speaks globally and his range of books is published in 44 languages. If we meet someone who introduces herself as a motivational speaker, she has to measure up to Robin and that's a big challenge. So, think of an introduction that is different and makes your brand distinct. Visit websites such as **www.siegerinternational.com**, and see how people advertise what they do. What do you like about it, what would you do differently? If you can say something different, that brief moment where the listener is wondering what your words mean will buy you the opportunity to arrange a meeting!

> ✍ **Exercise:**
>
> Instead of saying 'I'm an accountant', you could say, 'I grow money for companies'.
>
> Think of your brand message or 'elevator pitch' - how could you re-word it to make it more succinct and powerful?

● **Use your initiative**

We talked in the last section about asking sensible and clarifying questions but it is also really important to give relevant and accurate information in reply. We all know about the Charge of the Light Brigade – misinformation that got increasingly muddled with each messenger! When in doubt, write everything down, feed it back to the person giving the information to check it's correct, and then ensure the same paper is passed along.

> *'Don't be afraid to ask dumb questions:*
> *they're easier to handle than dumb mistakes.'*
>
> Anon

● **Avoid using dead-end statements**

For example, don't say such as, 'This has nothing to do with my department – please redial.' The customer wants a solution so use your initiative and ensure they get one by going the extra mile.

● **Patience**

Use endless patience – combined with a sense of humour and perspective. The reality is that, when you finish, you can go home to a good film, meal, or whatever. Focus on those things and it is easier to keep everything in perspective. A great skill is to let the person talk until he has said what he wants to say – if he is rude or objectionable, stop him firmly by saying, for example, 'I really want to hear what you have to say but I find your language upsetting. Can you please calm down and then continue'. If you are working for a call centre there are protocols in place to deal with this kind of thing but there is a good proverb which says, *'Do not walk in the way of evil men, avoid it, turn away from it and pass on.'* Proverbs 4:14,15

● **Empathy and humour**

Hear what people are saying but don't take it personally. You are just the sounding board for their personal journey – and if you encounter real idiots, don't drop your standards. As my mother always said – *'People who swear only do so because they have a poor command of English!'*

Golden Rule 26

Behind every grey cloud there is blue sky.

d) Selling a communication experience – example

Let's take an example based on experiences we've all had and see how they can be handled to create 'WOW' customer satisfaction.

Golden Rule 27

The customer isn't always right but we can act as if he or she might have been!

You've received a bill and it's wrong (from your point of view, even though the facts may be correct!). You call immediately and get through to the first of several options to press. Inadvertently you press the wrong button and have to start again. You scald yourself on the coffee you've poured to drink while calling so have to start again! You're now feeling aggrieved by the bill, sorry for your burnt lips and so press the first option button – which takes you to the wrong department. Instead of bills, you are through to 'New Customers'!

'Hello you're through to New Customers, how can I help you?'

At this point you let it all hang out, you're so grateful to have someone to talk to, they get the full monty – and you're not going to go back through the push button system to get the right place. So how can the staff member respond in a way which will creating the WOW communications experience which will result in your recommending their business to new clients?

Wow response (a)   *'You seem to have had quite a stressful time with all of this. Why don't I see if I can put you straight through to the right department. I'll let them know what the problem is and it should get sorted quite easily. Before I put you through, is there anything else we can help you with?'*

Wow response (b)   *'It sounds as this has been quite stressful for you. I think I can call your details up on my system, so* why don't I try and sort it for you – and if I can't, I'll put you straight through to the right department.'

Wow response (c)   (In the right department by this time and the bill was wrong). *'I can see where the error has happened so let me correct that right now. We'll refund that to your account. I do apologise for this mistake and am glad you called up about it. I'll re-issue an amended bill which will be with you in a couple of days.'*

(In the right department but the bill is correct and you are in the wrong). *'I can see how the bill might appear to have been more than you expected. It was good that you called up to double-check as sometimes there can be mistakes in billing. Is there anything else I can help you with? Don't hesitate to call at any time.'*

'Some days you're the dog and other days you're the hydrant.'
Anon

Chapter 6 – Exercise answer page

Exercise A

- I would like to look at how we could lift your game.

- Are you aware of the implications of your actions?

- What do you feel is affecting the smooth running of your team?

7

Cross-cultural Communication

'Hawaii is a unique state. It is a small state. It is a state that is by itself. It is a ... it is different from the other 49 states. Well, all states are different, but it's got a particularly unique situation.'

Dan Quayle, US Vice-President

I don't think Dan Quayle is alone in getting tongue-tied when put on the spot about a part of his country. Often tourists know more about our country than we do simply because they are interested enough to read up on a place before they visit it. However, there is a great deal of difference between holidaying in a country and doing business or living in one.

We may well be excellent communicators in our own language but cross-cultural communication has as much to do with body language, manners and behaviour, as it does with words. As most of the global business players have education systems where learning English is quite common, it makes for a double-edged sword. Life can be both easier and harder for businesses.

On the one hand we can be sufficiently proficient in a language to talk with people and they seem to understand what we are saying, but at the same time we can sometimes get the feeling that we've not quite communicated what we meant. When we lived in Germany my husband wanted to give me earrings for a birthday present and he duly walked me to the department store where he'd spotted the pair he wanted to buy - they were for pierced ears. I hate needles but thought this would be swift and painless. We approached the lady behind the earring counter and my husband asked if he could have his wife's ears pierced and used the word *'durchbohren'*. The woman looked quite shocked and then twigged what he meant - he had used the word for drilling instead of piercing!

Whether you are a company dealing with other countries or your work is mainly in the UK or your local area, there are principles in cross-cultural communication that, when understood, will be enormously beneficial. The best place to start are the different stages we go through when we engage in a different culture.

There are **five stages of cross-cultural adjustment** that every individual experiences to one degree or another when he or she gets involved in a different culture - whether working within Europe or somewhere in the rest of the world. It may also be patently obvious to many of you that working in a different area of the UK really can be like entering a different culture. For example, Glasgow (West coast) humour is quite distinct from Edinburgh (East coast) humour. We want to emphasise that whether you are moving from one job to another, one house to another, one country to another, you will experience culture change.

We lived in Germany for a couple of years and when we arrived back, a friend who had worked in India explained the five stages of cultural change which, if we'd known them before we went to Germany, would have explained everything.

'The whole object of travel is not to set foot on a foreign land; it is at last to set foot on one's own country as a foreign land.'
G K Chesterton

Communication skills can help you adjust to cultural differences, engage with hearts and minds and ultimately not just win new business, but new friends too!

✍ **Exercise:**

Rate yourself according to the following scale: 1 = low,
2 = below average, 3 = average, 4 = very good, 5 = excellent

How would you rate your cultural knowledge of your own country?

a)   Key tourist attractions   _____

b)   Best places to eat   _____

c)   Sites of archaeological interest   _____

d)   Visits to museums and art galleries   _____

e)   Best routes to scenic places   _____

f)   Famous writers/painters of the area   _____

g)   Gardens open to the public   _____

h)   Main post office location   _____

i)   Local public holidays   _____

j)   Type of humour!   _____

Understanding the Five Stages

Let's look at the five stages of cross-cultural change and see how they affect our communication effectiveness on the basis that the more relaxed we are, the easier it is to communicate and vice versa. We want to encourage you to step into the shoes of the other person, avoid behavioural gaffes and use knowledge of another language to create great working relationships

Honeymoon

The first stage is the **Honeymoon** - you arrive and everything is just so different. Doesn't the coffee smell so fresh, and look at how people just sit in the sunshine having breakfast and so on. Yes some things might be difficult to understand but really, we feel like we're on an extended holiday.

It's not too difficult trying the language as, if people don't understand, we can smile - and they tend to have some knowledge of English. On top of that, don't the business people dress in such a smart way and they have little fresh pastries with coffee in the office - so much better than anything we had back home.

It's also nice the way they like to really discuss each issue and isn't their English so good. It's amazing hearing them switch to their language to go much more in detail over our proposal - yes indeed this is going to be great for business. Then comes the second stage.

Rejection

All of a sudden it's not so easy to enjoy the cafes because we're really stressed. It's quite rude of them to talk in their own language and then give us pages of forms to fill out to help them decide on the proposal - and they're not in English!

Why do they want breakfast meetings at 7-00am - that's when we'd be getting up at home. Not only that, the milk tastes different and spoils the tea, and the breakfast cereal just isn't anything like we have at home. You might have thought we'd have got through the business quickly but they are making mountains out of molehills - these meetings are dragging on forever.

Back home we'd have had this done and dusted by now. Now it's not so nice when they switch language - they're probably saying something negative about our proposal. As for the coffee, any more caffeine and I'll have to be chained to the chair. Everything is relative.

'When you are courting a nice girl, an hour seems like a second. When you sit on a red-hot cinder, a second seems like an hour. That's relativity.'

Albert Einstein

Then, happily, we move to stage three.

Tolerance

What a wonderful word. Actually, when I think about it, doing business at home would have been just as protracted, I only have to remember that business with Kerploing & Co to get this situation in perspective.

'Every person takes the limits of their own field of vision for the limits of the world.'

Arthur Schopenhauer.

Now that I understand that the way they live and do business here isn't wrong, it's just different, life is getting easier. Going to the language class and trying more conversational opportunities, I'm picking up a lot more of what is being said - to think I was suspicious that they were being critical. Easy to see how paranoid we can get. Wish we could get some of this type of food back home. Must take some back for the family. This next stage is a great one.

Acceptance

I am really beginning to get used to how things are and feel like I am settling in. Things aren't so frustrating and in fact I'm beginning to understand where these people are coming from and why they act the way they do. I've enjoyed getting to know what makes them tick and it's a lot better since I've found my way round the town, e.g. the post office, how to ask for stamps or ask for the bill.

The language is getting easier and I even tried cracking a joke - they definitely have a different sense of humour but I didn't feel an idiot.

'The important thing ...is not so much to obtain new facts as to discover new ways of thinking about them.'

Sir William Bragg

This last stage is the best.

Embracement

At last, a sense of belonging and realising that these are people just like anyone else. I'm finally beginning to understand how this culture ticks and now I can really make a joke they laugh at. Friendships and relationships have enabled me to go deeper into the culture. I am now being accepted as someone who appreciates them for who they are and am not treated as the foreigner any more. I only wish I could help my boss back home learn to understand and appreciate the culture as I do - maybe he should try living in a different culture for a while.

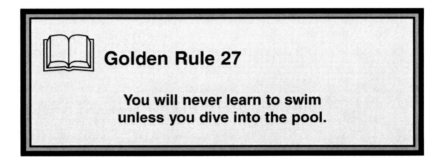

Golden Rule 27

You will never learn to swim unless you dive into the pool.

Cross-cultural communication

We wanted to give an overview of some of the key areas where cross cultural communication might cause problems - misunderstanding and offence amongst others, and at the same time see what can be used positively. The following sections look at two European cultures, Germany and France, and also America. Just because we speak a similar form of English doesn't mean we understand each other. What we will cover is very much generalisations - all fish swim in the sea but there are many types of fish - but they highlight what most people will experience to one degree or another.

Sample Cultures

Germany

The key things to identify about the German culture is that firstly they have a strong national identity - even though this has been challenged somewhat by the removal of the Berlin Wall - and they are also, despite the beach towels on the sun lounger reputation, very insecure!

> *'The Germans always buy platform tickets before they storm a railway station.'*
>
> Attributed to Lenin

They tend to be suspicious of everything and anything, and to that end have produced remarkable bureaucratic procedures to ensure every possible angle is covered - in short, angst about failure drives processes.

> *'What gives me angst is worrying about whether or not I ought to feel angst.'*
>
> German student quoted by John Ardagh

Crucial tips for working with Germans

1 **History:** Make an effort to understand their cultural heritage. Most older Germans find the First and Second World wars difficult to discuss but at the same time are very proud of the hard work involved in post-war rebuilding efforts. It's important to understand that today's younger generations carry a sense of embarrassment but at the same time want to be free of always being reminded of the past. The British on the other hand have always enjoyed reruns of 'Battle of Britain' without perhaps being so aware that this might appear as a lack of letting go of the past.

Whatever you do, don't fall into the famous Basil and Manuel behaviour in Fawlty Towers - trying to avoid something but mentioning it every time you open your mouth!

2 **Humour:** As the Germans are quite insecure, they have not got that British ability to laugh at themselves. One of the things that is great about the German language is that it says what it means. This does lead to very long words, for example, *heitere-gelassenheit* is simply cheerfully going with the flow - but it sounds great in German.

The English language is fantastic for wordplay and we can find a lot of fun just translating names into their real meaning, e.g. meeting Herr Kaltenbacher (cold stream) for lunch at a pub by a river might encourage us after a pint or so to ask if he has to run to the loo. This might amuse us but he wouldn't have a clue why we were laughing!

If we don't understand the different meanings of German words, we could do a John F Kennedy - in Berlin, when he said *'Ich bin ein Berliner,'* he should have said *'Ich bin Berliner'* - I am from Berlin. Someone should have quietly advised him that *ein Berliner* means a jam-filled doughnut! German humour is also either very visual or very wordy. For example the beginning of a joke would often be a long, dull rigmarole of background information and scene-setting, seemingly going on forever before even a hint of where the joke would lie. Who would want to wait around for the next five minutes before the punch line!!

3   **Desire for order:** Mostly anything that relates to life or living has a regulation to govern it. American friends had a visit from the police when their neighbour heard them drilling screws into the wall just one minute past 8pm. Complaints have been known against couples who left their child's pram on the lawn outside their own house, having a shower after 10pm or not putting the household rubbish for recycling into the five different bins - and on top of that, putting glass bottles into the bin after 8pm!!

When dealing with businesses, you need to respect their methodology even although it might seem old-fashioned, bureaucratic and over the top.

> *'Our firm has been functionally organised for the past 95 years.'*
>
> Answer to industrial survey

France

Like the Germans, the French have a strong sense of national identity ready to claim the superiority over other nations for art, food, philosophy and so on. There are some wonderful areas in France with warm and caring people. The cities, particularly Paris, like to keep foreigners at a distance and give the feeling that visitors are tolerated rather than embraced.

The French have an idealistic view of themselves and can be shocked when the unthinkable happens. In late 2005, for example, after berating the Americans for their intolerance towards Muslim countries, France experienced their worst three weeks of rioting - from racial tensions. Their post-revolution Liberty, Equality and Fraternity was severely tested and found wanting.

> *'If my theory of relativity is proven successful, Germany will claim me as a German and France will declare that I am a citizen of the world. Should my theory prove untrue, France will say that I am a German and Germany will declare that I am a Jew.'*
>
> Albert Einstein Address at the Sorbonne, Paris

Crucial Tips for working with the French

1 **Nationalism:** this can be seen as paranoia especially where language is concerned. There is a general dislike of any words sneaking into everyday vocabulary - for example, le hamburger - which smack of another culture. Any dilution of pure French is frowned upon so it is always best to use the French word for something where possible and relevant.

They can relish a good argument, refusing to admit to being wrong and don't care what you think of them. To their credit, the energy they put into being right, is also the same energy that enables them to be tenacious and innovative which is great for business. So when talking business, if you focus on these traits as positives, that makes for great outcomes.

The French also have distinct dialects which are all spoken very distinctly. Their love of their country, their language, food, way of life and so on means that they will launch verbal assaults on those who imply criticism of what is simply the best.

They have sharp intellects and really enjoy engaging in debate, often quite heated, without feeling any responsibility to accept that they might not be stating the truth. It is the verbal equivalent of entering the Coliseum with gladiatorial combats using brilliant mental skills rather than chariots. In business, this means that a foreign businessman can feel a discussion is either going really well, if they are holding their own, or really badly - if they are being taken down a philosophical maze.

Mood swings are part of the French psyche and if the mood in the room gets negative, then any deal has the potential to go sour, no matter how well it has been going until then. A break is required to restore emotional balance. If you're not ready for these swings, it can leave you feeling unsettled.

2 **Fair play:** this is a misnomer as the French only apply it to certain areas of society that don't affect the males' position or the possibility of being unsuccessful. It is difficult for women to achieve success without there being claims of bedroom derring-

do or some other underhand reason.

On the other hand, the French establishment finds it derisible that discipline issues, such as politicians having extra-marital affairs, in any way compromise a politician's plans for moving up the ladder. These apparent double standards also apply to the way in which many immigrant workers are treated, even if these are from another European country.

British people might generally find this quite shocking as, for example, we do genuinely want to break the 'glass ceiling' for women in business, and also encourage ethnic diversity. At any rate, as most of our underhand methods normally end up with front page press coverage, they are generally no longer hidden but in full public view!

'The English rely on their intuition and the French
on their grey matter.'

Anthony Burgess

3 **Individuality vs Creativity:** Knowledge is power for the French and so each person guards his or her individuality. This can make working in teams or on joint projects incredibly difficult. The advantage however is that the fantastically creative French flare for innovation will, through argument and brainstorming, eventually become common knowledge from which the team can benefit.

When working with a team of French people, you must not be put off by what may appear to be an aggressive style of communication, but show resilience as this will pay dividends. As the French love brilliant oratory, the cut and thrust of debate and argument, counter-argument and logic are their linguistic bread and butter.

For a British business person, there is the thrill of concluding a deal. For the French business person, the thrill is in the negotiation - analysing themes, philosophies, hypothetical outcomes and so on. The final deal is an anti-climax and so a Mexican stand-off can result.

America

The land of opportunity and freedom. The famous Statue of Liberty, provided by the French, reminds everyone that this is a land where all men are equal and anyone with an enterprising spirit can 'boldly go where no man has been before'. A melting pot of cultures where identity is dictated not by celebrating unity but diversity, hence African-American, Hispanic-American, Italian-American and so on.

A young country compared to any other civilisation, America has burgeoned in the last 250 years and assimilated ideas, philosophies and mindsets which at times are quite mind boggling. A country where less than 20% of the population have a passport and even less have ever travelled outside the States, their world view is based on a very insular knowledge base - and the internet.

Yet American writers, speakers and business leaders dictate the new trends and thinking on the global business platform. They are very self-protective and President Bush's policies in protecting oil and petrol have reinforced this image. Jonathon Porritt of Friends of the Earth described President Bush as having undone in one term of office, the last 35 years' advances in repairing the environment.

'I have opinions of my own - strong opinions - but I don't always agree with them.'
President George W Bush

1 **Social rituals:** The experience we have of Americans in business is based on established social rituals. Body language is very open, with back-slapping, big smiles, firm handshakes and a generally warm and winsome approach. They are very much 'in your face' and will want to have your email address and phone number, and invite you to meet up at some point. They never will call and if you met again would go through the same ritual of back-slapping, big smiles, firm handshakes and say how time has gone by and you really must get that lunch at some point.

   The reality is that while some might mean what they say at the time, in general, they have no intention of following through. What is important is that they have done all the right social signals. This is very powerful when it comes to winning deals as the Americans come across as confident, capable and will win hearts and minds at an early stage. The fact that their expertise doesn't necessarily have the quality of delivery is secondary.

   As stated earlier in the book, people buy you, not your product, and this warm confidence (despite its shallowness) is very influential. An Austrian friend was at a conference in the States and, as he waited in the venue foyer, an American businessman came over and introduced himself with the usual ritual handshakes and so on. He asked my friend, 'How are you?' to which my friend described a very painful bereavement he had just experienced. Someone else caught the American's attention and with a, 'Well, have a nice day!' he was off to the next back-slapping encounter.

   In general, depth of relationships is not one of their strengths and so that makes their level of communication superficial. The key thing is to take it at that level and have low expectations of developing genuine relationships with people whilst at the same time enjoy the whole bonhomie that goes with their culture.

   They are very innovative, open to enjoying life and genuinely want people to feel happy - and they have produced great comedians!

'From the moment I picked your book up until I laid it down, I was convulsed with laughter. Some day I intend reading it.'
Groucho Marx

2 **Honesty:** Whilst superficiality in relationships is a hallmark of the American culture, it is also true to say they love honesty. When it comes to getting things done, they are fantastic with a real 'can-do' approach. An American friend who works in negotiations in the UK was at her first meeting and the deal was, for her, getting quite frustrating. Various heads of departments representing the client were pontificating and she eventually just dealt with it American style by asking whether they were going to 'piss or get off the pot'. There was a stunned silence and the meeting was brought to a close. The next day her boss asked her to call the other individuals to apologise. They responded with laughter and said it was the best thing that could have happened and they signed the deal there and then!

   Americans don't like to beat around the bush so if you're wanting to talk business, just be direct. One thing to beware of is how you react while someone is talking. For example, if an American is sharing a proposal or discussing their suggestion, avoid nodding your head and saying 'yes' in agreement to what they are saying as you go along. For them 'yes' means you have made a firm business commitment to what they are selling/proposing when all you are saying is, 'I hear what you are saying at this moment.'

3 **Can-do:** There is no such thing as an obstacle for an American and what really frustrates them is when they are faced by negative communication. This is a country that has a pioneer background and still holds to its right to bear weapons - a wild west mentality. It is also very hard on the poor as, if you don't succeed, it is your responsibility and so the rich are rich and the poor have a very

hard time. Material success is what gives credibility and so they are very challenged by getting older.

'I was fired because of my age. I'll never make the mistake of being seventy again.'

Casey Stengel

In business, cosmetic surgery for young businessmen (up to 40 years of age) has increased dramatically in the last few years as fear of looking older raises the spectre of being replaced by a younger person! Can-do sounds great but it is driven by a fear of not looking eternally young, by not being able to retire with financial security and fear of the cost of being ill.

Whilst the British may not have a can-do approach, we have a healthier (if more fatalistic) and less competitive view of life. We can appreciate someone for who they are rather than what they have and this is very valuable in business.

Other cultural pot-holes to avoid

This small book does not have the capacity to consider all the possible inter-cultural gaffes that you can make in your dealings with foreigners, but a couple of examples can give a taste of the problems that can be encountered.

When receiving business cards from **Chinese** colleagues, always take them with both hands (they will be offered with both hands), and look at them carefully, making some complimentary remark. A noted British academic received a Chinese delegation with a view to inter-university cooperation, folded the leader's proffered card in two and slipped it under the glass top of his desk with barely a glance. The delegation walked out and no deal was ever done. The card is an immediate representation of the status and worth of the giver. Remember this!

Be aware that the **Japanese**, whilst being extremely polite and listening carefully and quietly to your presentation, will be absorbing every detail and nuance, missing nothing. They may not ask questions at the time but will invite you to join them later in the sushi bar and analyses every aspect.

For the **Israelis**, humour is essential in business, but not at the first meeting – because it might come across as lacking in sincerity. Their humour is not very easy to grasp and, if in doubt, just forget about it. Once a bond is created, it may be for life, and long-term business is conducted as real friends, but to get there may take longer than swimming the Atlantic.

An American colleague who had been working with troops in Iraq tells of a paranoid Lt Colonel who always makes sure he sits with his back straight, on the edge of his chair, boots flat on the ground, right hand gripping left wrist, when talking with local leaders. The necessity to adopt local habits and etiquette is vital, as the opportunities to offend are legion. Just imagine entering an **Iraqi** sheik's house, giving him and assembled male relatives a vigorous, iron-grip handshake, declining his offer of tea with a dismissive wave of your left hand, but accepting a bowl of nuts with a thumbs-up gesture and scooping up nuts with the left hand, sitting with your ankle over your knee and looking around the room, bereft of women, and asking the sheik, 'So, how's your wife?' You cannot get more wrong that all that!

To pursue these themes further, see *'Business Chameleon'* by Ron Roet and Diana Beaver, published by Management Books 2000.

✍ **Exercise:**

1   Which cultures have you experienced?

2   Which of the five stages can you identify most with?

3   List the key qualities of the culture you visit most?

4   What do you appreciate and what do you dislike?

5   How do you think you come across to others?

8

And Finally

Throughout the book, we have highlighted a number of golden rules. By regularly reviewing and practicing these rules you will find the key to successful communication.

Summary of Golden Rules

Golden Rule 1   **It is better to say nothing, than to witter, unless of course you can witter with conviction!**

Golden Rule 2   **It is better to smile and relax than be lax with your smile!**

Golden Rule 3   **Ask who, what, why, where and when questions to save misunderstandings – better a meeting of meaning than a clash of attitudes !**

Golden Rule 4   **When in doubt, miss it out!**

Golden Rule 5   **Never underestimate the power of the written word.**

Golden Rule 6	**Never use straw when you can use paper.**
Golden Rule 7	**He who avoids being pedantic shows great wisdom.**
Golden Rule 8	**Better to break down your sentences than give your readers a breakdown!**
Golden Rule 9	**Let your personality smile through your pen.**
Golden Rule 10	**It is easier to make friends than enemies.**
Golden Rule 11	**When you are networking work your net.**
Golden Rule 12	**Use networking to grow your circle of contacts and friends.**
Golden Rule 13	**It is as important to give as it is to receive in networking.**
Golden Rule 14	**See colleagues as friends and allies.**
Golden Rule 15	**Relationships are the key to happiness and success.**
Golden Rule 16	**Take control of your electronic communication before it takes control of you.**
Golden Rule 17	**Do to others what you'd like them to do for you email-wise.**
Golden Rule 18	**Your voicemail can open or close doors.**

Golden Rule 19	Prepare, observe and act!
Golden Rule 20	The personal touch is the only way to touch the person, i.e. they buy you, not the product
Golden Rule 21	The way you treat your people is the model they will adopt for treating others.
Golden Rule 22	Avoid being a 'lemon-sucker' – it makes your words wrinkled and sour!
Golden Rule 23	If you make the world a nicer place to live in, you'll enjoy living in it too!
Golden Rule 24	When being honest, it is always better to sound like a flute player than a drummer.
Golden Rule 25	He who speaks acid words will eventually burn his tongue.
Golden Rule 26	Behind every grey cloud there is blue sky.
Golden Rule 27	The customer isn't always right but we can act as if he or she might have been!
Golden Rule 28	You will never learn to swim unless you dive into the pool.

Appendix 1
A Simple Theory of Communication

Searching through the available literature on the science (or art?) of communication can be a daunting task – there is so much to see. However, embracing all of it is one quintessentially simple theory which can be best illustrated by a diagram.

This book bears witness to the necessity of making things crystal clear when writing, talking, listening-and-interpreting, gesturing, showing or whatever method of passing on information you choose. This approach is just as important for the man on the deck of the aircraft carrier with his semaphore flags as it is for the Governor of the Bank of England explaining why he chooses to raise the interest rate again; or for the native Australian talking to his ancestors as much as for the rescuer talking to the woman trapped under fallen masonry after an earthquake.

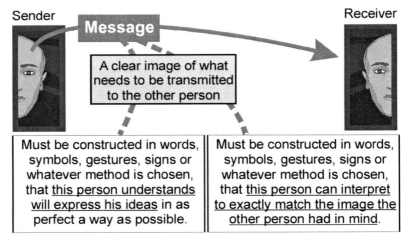

Figure – Alexander's theory of communication

The figure shows that several things **must take place** for communication to be effective.

● The sender (speaker, writer, signaller and so on) must have a clear idea of what the message should be. This involves having a precise image of the idea, whether in words or pictures or whatever.

● The sender must be able to construct the message in a style that exactly describes that image.

● *(Possibly the most important bit for the accurate transfer of the message)* The receiver (listener, reader, sensor) must have the same level of understanding of the symbols, words or pictures that the sender uses, in order to construct **exactly the same image** in his or her brain.

Take a simple example – a bloke in a bar wants to order a couple of pints of lager, but the crowd around the bar is some two or three deep. He has several options:

1. He can stick two fingers up in the air when (and if) the barman catches his eye, and then make a drinking gesture with his other hand.

2. He can ask someone in the crowd to pass his message forward to the barman.

3. He can go thirsty.

4. He can catch the barman's eye and call out, *'Two pints of Stella please, in straight glasses.'*

The first option is likely to get short shrift and possibly a poke in the eye from someone nearby who misinterprets the first gesture. Even if the barman sees the gestures, it is not clear what the chap wants two of – could be anything from pints of best to tequila sunrises.

The second option is like the old game of Chinese whispers and will never result in service – especially if it seeks to take advantage of others waiting.

The third is not tenable.

The final one is clearly the best as the image in the drinker's head (two Stellas in straights) is very precise and can easily be interpreted/transmitted in words. The barman, being an expert in such matters will have exactly the same understanding of the words and will react with a perfect image in his head. Unless the crowd rebels, the drinker should get his drinks.

> **Note** – the drinker will probably know that a 'straight' is the local word for a glass without a handle. This is worth checking as part of the message compilation. Similarly, local custom talks about 'pot', 'mug', 'handle', 'tankard' or a myriad other colloquial words for the other sort, the one with a handle. Strange lot, drinkers!

Essential facts

Many communications fail because the sender of the message fails to choose the right way to imagine and express it – and does not check that the receiver can perform the same analysis. There is a strange arrogance in many people which seems to suggest that they are experts in communicating – *'I know what I mean – are you stupid or something?'*

Have you ever asked a computer-literate colleague to explain something that you cannot fathom on your computer? (Or have you asked a ten-year old?) Chances are he or she will know the answer and will show you with flying fingers and a wealth of technobabble that leaves you gasping for breath. Suggest that the expert treats you like a five-year old and starts again but at quarter speed so that you can write the answer down as it is demonstrated. What you are doing is ensuring that the bottom right-hand box on the diagram is being complied with – that the receiver has the ability to interpret the message exactly. (We cannot doubt the sender's ability to image the answer correctly and use the right words and actions.)

So, to summarise, the essential facts are:

1. **Be clear what you want to send.**

2. **Choose the perfect way to send it.**

3. **Be sure that the receiver will understand it.**

And mine is a pint of Old Speckled Hen, please, in a mug.

There was an interesting variation on this 1-2-3 pattern shown on television recently. An elderly householder had been defrauded out of several thousand pounds by a rogue financial advisor. He achieved *his* objective in gaining access to her money – he had a clear image and used the right words. She was hard of hearing and didn't completely understand what he was saying, consequently signing away funds, believing that he was trustworthy. The guy was a right villain and, if he had used 1, 2 <u>and 3</u> as he should, the old lady would never have signed and he would have been sent away with a flea in his ear. By not engaging with number 3, he had breached the etiquette necessary for correct and decent communications, for his own nefarious ends.

It could be argued, within this theory of communicating, that there is equal responsibility placed on the sender *and* the receiver to make sure that the telling is effectively completed. Fair enough – but as the sending tends to happen before the receiving, the greater onus is on the sender to check that the other person has the skills and knowledge to make sense of the message.

So, communicators beware!

Is that clear?!

James Alexander